D1744542

GIMME
THE
RECIPE

SHEILA
KIELY

MERCIER PRESS

80003336798

I dedicate this book to my
home-grown team of testers,
helpers and critics:
my husband Denis
and my children Johnnie,
Ellie, Dáire, Eimear, Niall
and Denny.

Northamptonshire Libraries & Information Service
BH

Askews & Holts	

CONTENTS

INTRODUCTION

If you are like me, then most days you are running around like a mad thing playing catch up with everything. **Shower, dress and eat. Wash on, wash out, wash up. Kids up, kids fed, kids out. Work, sleep and repeat.** Somewhere in between you have to manage the school run, housework and grocery shopping, and what were you thinking when you invited people over for dinner at the weekend? That mound of ironing will not iron itself, so you will have to hide it. Neither will those sheets walk off the beds and make their own way to the washing machine, so you will have to bribe one of the kids to change them, and speaking of kids, what on earth are you going to feed them for dinner tonight?

Deep breath. Relax.

By midweek, we are all to varying degrees busy, surviving, stressed, frustrated, tired, frazzled, bewildered, bothered and living for the weekend. I know what it is like to parade up and down the overflowing aisles of the supermarket and not have a clue what I want. I'm sure you know the feeling – your head is wrecked and you are not in the humour for grappling with steering the shopping trolley away from a small child who thinks it is hilarious to bash into other trolleys. You want to serve up something that is easy to prepare, well-balanced and nutritious, but that does not take too long to cook – in my case for six hungry kids. It sounds like a lofty ambition, but it doesn't have to be as hard as you imagine.

The idea for this book came about by chance. A few times a week I try to go for a run with my friend Deirdre, both to clear my head and to work off the brownies, and she often asks me for ideas for what she can cook for dinner. It was this that inspired me to pull together all my everyday recipes so I would have a stockpile of easily accessible solutions to the perennial problem of what to make for the hungry family. Then I realised that there are probably lots of people out there in the same boat as Deirdre and myself, so I decided to compile my recipes into a book, with the aim of helping other busy parents who need something straightforward to cook that is healthy, filling and made from readily available ingredients. I came up with the title for the book very easily – *Gimme the Recipe* – as this is what I say to my friends and what they say to me when we are sharing recipes. With work on the book underway, I attended a Food Writer's course at Ballymaloe with John and Sally McKenna. It was Sally who encouraged us all to

start blogging as a way to break into the food writing world – I honestly didn't know what blogging was before that! The day after the Food Writer's course I started my blog and www.gimmetherecipe.com was born in February 2010. The positive response to my blog encouraged me in my quest to have my book published.

The book has been laid out in the way that food features in my lifestyle. The main section is to answer the 'What's for dinner Mom?' question. Monday to Friday cooking is often done under pressure and during a busy week there is little time for experimentation or planning in the kitchen, so this section offers the most recipes.

Next up, the section 'Baking Day' presents recipes you can enjoy cooking in your leisure time.

Finally 'Dinner Party (and other special occasions)' is for those rare times when you put in a bit more time and effort to produce a dish with a bit of finesse. However, this doesn't mean it has to be a terribly complicated culinary masterpiece and I have tried to keep the recipes in this section relatively simple, but with results that will still impress the guests.

In the final part of the book, 'Planning Family Gatherings and Parties at Home', I have provided easy to follow plans to take the stress out of catering for a crowd, including Christmas Dinner. These should help you prepare for and plan big events in advance, allowing you more time on the day to actually enjoy yourself.

I have always had an interest in food, but am a very long way from being a professional chef. I have chosen the recipes for this book bearing in mind that none of us have a trained chef in our kitchen. When we cook, most of us gather ingredients, throw them onto the worktop, pull out the chopping board, pots and pans, put on the apron and then start to cook. We do not prepare things in little bowls for assembly cooking, instead we prepare as we go. With this in mind, I have written the ingredients in order of use and the method to include the preparation as part of the cooking process.

I hope that my approach is practical and not preachy. I am all for healthy eating, but, as with everything in life, we all need to spoil ourselves sometimes – there is no room for guilt at my table.

Enjoy,

Sheila

USEFUL KITCHEN EQUIPMENT

You do not need lots of fancy equipment to make my dishes, but the right tools will help and for me they include the following:

- Accurate weighing scales (I use a digital scales): all measurements listed are metric so please see the conversion table if you need to convert to imperial
- Measuring jugs: one of up to a litre capacity and one small jug for measuring up to 250ml
- Measuring spoons: 1 tbsp, 1 tsp, ½ tsp, ¼ tsp
- Wooden spoons
- Spatula
- Electric mixer with beater, whisk and dough hook attachment
- Tower grater with three or four different-sized graters on each side for cheese and onions, etc.
- Handheld fine microplane grater for ginger, nutmeg, etc.
- Garlic crusher
- Lemon zester and juicer (I use an old-fashioned wooden juicer)
- Blender

- Mini chopper or food processor (I don't yet own a food processor and use a mini chopper for whizzing things like breadcrumbs, Thai paste, pesto, etc., and chopping onions)
- Good chopping knives
- Chopping boards
- Mixing bowls
- Baking trays and dishes
- Cupcake trays
- Cake tins – sandwich tins, spring-form release
- 2lb loaf tin (yes, I know I'm a metric girl, but this is how they're sold)
- Casserole pots – large (I love my Jamie Oliver Professional Pot Roast and cast-iron Le Creuset Casserole Pot)
- Sieve
- Rolling pin

Of all of the above equipment, a good electric mixer is a great investment if you are going to do a lot of baking. My mother gave me her Kenwood Major and it has being going strong since the mid 1980s.

CONVERSION TABLES

DRY INGREDIENTS

Metric	Imperial
5 grams	⅛ ounce
10g	¼oz
15g	½oz
20g	¾oz
25g	1oz
50g	2oz
75g	3oz
100-125g	4oz
150g	5oz
175g	6oz
200g	7oz
225g	8oz
250g	9oz
275g	10oz
300g	11oz
325g	12oz
350g	13oz
400g	14oz
425g	15oz
450g	1lb
1kg (1000g)	2¼lb

LIQUIDS

Metric	Imperial
25ml	1 fluid ounce
50	2
75	3
125	4
150	5
175	6
200	7
225	8
250	9
275	10
500ml	0.87 pint
1 litre (1000ml)	1.75 pints
American cup	8 fluid ounces
Small glass	150ml

OVEN HEAT AND TEMPERATURES

Most electric ovens are multi-purpose and will have a fan-assisted setting and this is what I use. I find it is better to use this setting as it distributes the heat around the oven for more even, faster cooking than a conventional oven. If you use a conventional oven you will need to increase the temperature by approximately 20–25 degrees and the cooking time will be a little longer. (You will need to consult your cooker manual for this, as ovens will vary.)

Note: Fan ovens are also known as 'convectional' as opposed to 'conventional' traditional ovens.

TEMPERATURES

All oven temperatures given are in Celsius and are for fan-assisted ovens. The equivalent Gas Mark temperature is also given.

TEMPERATURE CONVERSION TABLE

Fan Oven Celsius	Conventional Oven	Gas Mark	Fahrenheit
90°C (Very cool)	110°C	¼	225°F
110°C	130°C	½	266°F
120°C (Cool)	140°C	1	284°F
130°C	150°C	2	302°F
140°C (Moderate)	160°C	3	320°F
150°C	170°C	3	338°F
160°C	180°C	4	356°F
170°C (Mod. Hot)	190°C	5	374°F
180°C	200°C	6	392°F
190°C	210°C	6	410°F
200°C (Hot)	220°C	7	428°F
210°C	230°C	8	450°F
220°C (Very Hot)	240°C	9	464°F

FOOD SAFETY

The following food safety tips are important if you want to avoid making anybody sick:

- Wash your hands before beginning food preparation and wash your hands in between dealing with 'raw' and 'ready-to-eat' food so that you do not spread bacteria from one food to another, i.e. cross contamination.
- Raw meat and poultry should be stored below any 'ready-to-eat foods' in the fridge. No blood drip should be allowed to make contact with other food or food contact surfaces.
- Use different chopping boards and knives for preparing raw meat and poultry and other foods or at least wash the board and knife with very hot water and washing-up liquid before using for another purpose.
- The fridge should be kept at a temperature of 0 °C to +5°C.
- Cooked food should reach a temperature of +75°C before it is eaten. Cooking to the correct temperature will kill any harmful bacteria. This should be the core temperature of the food, so if you are cooking something particularly thick, such as a joint of beef, use a temperature probe to make sure.
- Be particularly careful when cooking minced meat. Make sure it is cooked on a high temperature, browned right through and that the juices run clear.
- Eating high-risk foods – primarily meat, dairy and salads items – that have been left unrefrigerated for more than thirty minutes between the temperatures of +5°C and +63°C could make you sick, as bacteria grows in between these temperatures.
- Wash fruit and vegetables and rinse herbs before you use them.
- If you are reheating a meal, reheat it to +70°C. Reheated food needs to be piping hot. Only reheat a meal once.
- Do not cook stuffing in the cavity of poultry, but in a separate dish.
- Keep the handles of your fridge, taps, cupboards, etc., clean.
- Leftovers, e.g. cooked poultry, should be used within three days of cooking.

NOTE ON ALLERGENS:

- The prevalence of food allergies is on the rise and there are currently fourteen listed food allergens – that means that they have to be indicated on the labelling of pre-packaged foods. Allergic reactions can be extremely severe and life threatening. Egg, nuts and gluten in particular are ingredients that can be somewhat hidden in the food we serve and is something that we need to be aware of e.g. ground almonds in a curry, pine nuts in pesto, flour as a thickener in a sauce, raw eggs in a chocolate mousse. For more information on Food Allergens, see www.safefood.eu.

STORE CUPBOARD, FREEZER AND FRIDGE LIST

The theory is if you stock up with half or even a quarter of the items from each group below, you will always be able to make a decent meal.

- *Fresh*: fruit and vegetables, fresh herbs such as basil and coriander, garlic, ginger, chillies, tortilla wraps, pitta breads.
- *Dried Herbs and Spices*: ground cumin, ground coriander, chilli powder, cayenne, paprika, oregano, turmeric, thyme, parsley, herbes de Provence, rosemary, whole black peppercorns and sea salt flakes.
- *Tinned*: chopped and plum tomatoes, tomato puree, chickpeas, kidney and baked beans, sweetcorn, coconut

milk, peaches, pears.
- *Dried*: pasta, rice, lentils, porridge oats, plain flour, self-raising flour, wholemeal flour, strong flour, bread soda, baking powder, caster sugar, icing sugar, brown sugar, fast-action bread yeast sachets (7g), raisins, apricots.
- *Dairy*: unsalted butter, milk, buttermilk, crème fraiche, double cream, a variety of hard and soft cheese such as cheddar, Parmesan and cream cheese, natural yoghurt.
- *Frozen*: chicken breasts, steak mince, stewing beef, peas, green beans, sweetcorn, ready to use filo and puff pastry sheets, mixed berries.
- *Other*: eggs, olive oil, sunflower

oil, balsamic vinegar, honey, Dijon and wholegrain mustard, vegetable, chicken and beef stock cubes, ground and flaked almonds, pine nuts, hazelnuts, vanilla extract, crackers, chocolate (50%+ cocoa content). Or you could just buy the chocolate …

NOTES ON INGREDIENTS:

- *Salt*: My preference is to use sea salt flakes in a salt grinder. I try not to add a lot of salt to my recipes and find that where herbs are used they impart enough flavour, removing the need for any extra seasoning.
- *Butter*: I use unsalted butter in both cooking and baking.

- *Stock*: I've managed to make home-made stock only a handful of times (shame on me) and usually use low-salt, organic stock cubes.

NOTE ON PORTION SIZE:

- The serving sizes given are generous adult-sized portions. A nice guideline from Safefood, when it comes to healthy eating and portion sizes, is to have a tennis ball size of starchy foods and a palm sized portion of protein. (That would be your palm, not Muhammad Ali's!)

WHAT'S FOR DINNER MOM?

WHAT'S FOR DINNER MOM?

I've been contemplating putting up a blackboard in our kitchen to write up 'Today's Special', because sometimes I just don't want to have to answer the question **'What's for Dinner Mom?'** With six children it's impossible to please all of them all of the time, and occasionally I get fed up hearing the moaning or seeing the crumpled face that implies I may as well be stirring a witch's cauldron!

What I have attempted to do in this section is provide a selection of recipes that are varied, balanced and suitable for everyday family dining, using ingredients that are readily available in the local supermarket. Varying the type of meal you cook will keep things interesting, i.e. if it's traditional one night, make it Italian the next.

I generally decide what's for dinner based on what we have had over the past few days. For example if we've already had chicken or pork during the week, then I would try to make a fish, beef or vegetarian dish. This section of the book is divided accordingly.

Dinner does not always have to mean meat and two vegetables. I will bet if you look in your fridge, you will have the makings of a tapas night or smorgasbord selection without any need to go to a shop. Keep your leftovers, even if it is only enough for one portion. Leftover Bolognese can be transformed into a filling for some potato skins topped with cheese. Leftover stew can become Cornish pasties. Cooked potatoes could be used to make a frittata or leftover cooked chicken could be used in soup. Make use of your freezer. A single portion of lasagne will make a welcome snack after a sports' training session for a hungry teenager.

In our house, when the kids were very small, Friday night was traditionally takeaway night and I now try to recreate that with an Indian curry, a spicy Thai dish or a pizza made at home. Recipes for these are in the DIY Takeaway section. Do not get me wrong here though, I do still order in the odd takeaway.

In case of emergencies (cupboards bare, time very limited), turn to the Super Quick Snacks and Dinners section, where there is a selection of recipes that can be whipped up very quickly. Remember the simple things, e.g. a baked potato with baked beans may not take long to prepare and cook, but it is still a nutritious and filling meal.

Finally, I suggest getting your older kids to help with the cooking of dinner – before long they will be capable of cooking by themselves. It would be nice if the answer to 'What's for Dinner Mom?' one day could become, 'I don't know, it's your night to cook.'

MUSHROOM SOUP

This is a hearty, warming soup to wrap your hands around and savour. One of these fine days I might make my own stock, but for now I use a low salt, organic stock cube from the supermarket. I like to use a combination of beef and vegetable stock to bring a bit more depth to this soup.

Method:

- Peel and finely chop the onion. Peel and crush the garlic. Wash the mushrooms and then chop into small pieces and set aside.
- Melt the butter in a large saucepan over a low heat and cook the onion for 5 minutes until soft.
- Turn the heat up to medium, add the chopped mushrooms and cook for 2 minutes, mixing well.
- Add the crushed garlic and cook for 1 minute.
- Rinse, finely chop and add the parsley with the beef and vegetable stocks, and bring the soup to the boil. Reduce the heat to simmer for 20 minutes and then use a blender to blend the soup.
- Serve with some fresh crusty bread.

Ingredients: – serves 4

1 small onion

1 garlic clove

200g mixed mushrooms

25g unsalted butter
    (approx. 1 heaped tbsp)

Small handful of fresh flat-leaf
    parsley

250ml beef stock

500ml vegetable stock

TIP: For extra richness try adding some cream when blending the soup or swirl it on top when serving.

* Tomatoes are acidic by nature. The riper they are the less acidic they will be. Some recipes add sugar to counter the acidity of tomatoes which will sweeten the dish and while it will taste less acidic, sugar does not actually reduce the acidity level of tomatoes. According to a little research I have done there are a couple of solutions that will reduce the acidity level if acid in your diet causes stomach problems. The first one is to add a little baking soda towards the end of cooking — this may taint the taste of the dish. The second, more pleasant suggestion is to serve the dish with grated cheese — the calcium in the cheese will neutralise the acidity somewhat. When I was little my mom used to always add milk to our tomato soup and a big swirl of cream should help too. Alternatively drinking a glass of milk as you eat your tomato-based meal would be an easy way to introduce some calcium too.

SEMI-SUN-DRIED CHERRY TOMATO SOUP

Soup gives warmth and comfort and it will keep in the fridge for a few days, so it's a perfect standby for a starving child who can't wait until dinner's ready. Semi-sun-dried tomatoes are readily available in the chilled cabinet of the supermarket and are usually marinated in a combination of oil and herbs. My local does a cherry tomato version and they are lovely and sweet. They add a rich maturity to the soup, but if you cannot get hold of them just leave them out and substitute with 2 tablespoons of tomato puree.

Method:

- Peel and crush the garlic.
- Melt the butter in a large saucepan over a low heat and cook the garlic for 1 minute until soft.
- Chop up the semi-sun-dried tomatoes as small as you can and add these with the canned plum tomatoes, vegetable stock, sugar and dried basil.
- Roughly chop up the plum tomatoes in the pan.
- Turn the heat up and bring the soup to the boil, then reduce the heat and simmer for 20 minutes.
- Use a blender to blend the soup.

Ingredients: – serves 4–5

2 garlic cloves

25g unsalted butter
(approx. 1 heaped tbsp)

120g semi-sun-dried cherry
tomatoes in oil

2 x 400g cans of plum tomatoes*

500ml vegetable stock

1 tsp sugar

1 tsp dried basil

TIPS: This soup is great served with some crunchy croutons on top. If you have any soup left over it makes a great pasta sauce.

Note: To make some easy home-made croutons, cube some crusty bread and place on a baking tray. Drizzle generously with olive oil and bake in a hot oven, tossing once during baking. Bake until crisp and brown.

CHICKEN SOUP

Chicken soup is like dinner in a bowl, but without the hard work of cutting and chewing. This is the soup that you need when you are feeling under the weather and in need of TLC. When you've finished a chicken dinner you may not think that there's much chicken left on the carcass, but salvage what you can and if you turn the chicken over there will be lots of moist tender pieces to pick off underneath; put these into a bowl and store in the fridge to make chicken soup the next day. I do not recommend blending chicken soup as you can end up with a very grainy texture.

Method:

- Peel and finely chop the onion and peel and dice the carrot.
- Melt the butter in a saucepan over a low heat, add the finely chopped onion and carrot, and cook for 5 minutes.
- Add the stock, thyme and chicken pieces and bring to the boil, then reduce the heat and simmer for 20 minutes.
- Serve with brown bread or crackers.

Ingredients: – serves 5

1 medium onion

1 large carrot

25g unsalted butter
(approx. 1 heaped tbsp)

1½ litres chicken stock

2 tsp dried thyme

300g leftover cooked chicken
pieces

TOMATO AND ROASTED RED PEPPER SOUP

Roasting red peppers is simple and once you have peeled the skins off you are left with wonderfully soft, almost sweet strips of pepper that can be used hot or cold. Blended into this soup they give it a warming yet sweet kick. Preparing the peppers is a bit of a fiddly process and not for when you are rushed. You can buy jars of roasted peppers if you do not have time to roast them yourself.

Method:

- Preheat the oven to 200°C/Gas Mark 7 and roast the whole red peppers until the skin becomes black and charred – this should take around 25 minutes. When they are blackened, place into a plastic sandwich bag or a bowl covered with cling film and allow to cool. The trapped steam will have softened the skin and made it very easy to peel off; then deseed and roughly chop them.
- Meanwhile, finely chop the onion and crush the garlic.
- Melt the butter in a large saucepan over a low heat and cook the onion for 5 minutes until soft.
- Add the crushed garlic, thyme and cinnamon, and cook for 1 minute.
- Add the chopped tomatoes and cook for 1 minute.
- Add the stock and bring to the boil then reduce the heat, add the chopped peppers and simmer for 20 minutes.
- Use a food processor to blend the soup.
- Serve with crispy bread rolls or toasted sandwiches.

Ingredients: – serves 5

2 red peppers

1 medium onion

1 garlic clove

25g unsalted butter
(approx. 1 heaped tbsp)

1 tsp dried thyme

½ tsp ground cinnamon

1 x 400g can of chopped tomatoes

750ml vegetable stock

TIP: Roast a couple of extra red peppers and store them whole in a jar of olive oil with some garlic and herbs to use as a delicious addition to a toasted sandwich or as a pizza topping.

SPICED CARROT, PARSNIP AND RED CHILLI SOUP

Carrots and parsnips make great partners and when they are getting past their best they can be rescued by whizzing them up into a soup and given extra warmth with the addition of a chilli. This is a perfect mid-winter warmer.

Method:

- Peel and cube the potato. Deseed and finely chop the red chilli.
- Melt the butter in a saucepan over a low heat, add the cubed potato, and cook for 2 minutes.
- Add the ground coriander and chopped chilli, stir well and cook for 1 minute.
- Meanwhile, peel and chop the carrots and parsnips and add them to the pan. Stir well, then add the vegetable stock and water, and bring to the boil.
- Reduce the heat and simmer for 20 minutes until the vegetables are just tender.
- Blend and serve with some spiced crunchy pitta chips (see p. 197).

Ingredients: – serves 4–5

1 medium potato

1 red chilli

25g unsalted butter
   (approx. 1 heaped tbsp)

2 tsp ground coriander

5 large carrots

2 large parsnips

750ml vegetable stock

250ml water

TIP: To deseed a chilli I cut the top off, slice it in half lengthways and use a teaspoon to scrape out the seeds and white pith.

CARROT AND CORIANDER SOUP

As I work from home, I love the days when I wander down to the fridge for lunch and find a bowl of leftover soup – this doesn't happen often. The sweetness of the carrots blends beautifully with the coriander in this now classic combination. Freshly chopped coriander is a great addition to this soup; however, it can be hard to source at times and the soup will stand up just as well if made using only the ground coriander.

Method:

- Peel and finely chop the onion. Peel and cube the potato and set aside.
- Melt the butter in a saucepan over a low heat, add the chopped onion, and cook for 5 minutes until soft.
- While the onion is softening, peel and chop the carrots.
- Add the cubed potato and the ground coriander to the onions, and cook for 1 minute.
- Add the carrots to the soup base along with the stock and bring to the boil.
- Cover and simmer for 20 minutes.
- Rinse and chop some of the fresh coriander (about a handful) and blend with the soup in a food processor or blender until smooth.
- Serve with some fresh crusty bread and a sprinkling of chopped fresh coriander.

Ingredients: – serves 5–6

1 medium onion

1 medium potato

25g unsalted butter
(approx. 1 heaped tbsp)

10 medium carrots
(approx. 1kg)

1 tsp ground coriander

1 litre vegetable stock

Small bunch of fresh coriander

TIP: Make a meal of soup by serving it with some stuffed baked potatoes (see p. 35) or toasted ham and cheese sandwiches.

CHUNKY CARROT AND CHILLI BEAN STEW

This is a deep-filled bowl of comfort. A warming and highly nutritious chunky winter soup, served with crusty bread, this is a meal in itself. It could feature as a rustic dinner party mains for a casual supper served with crackers and a good Irish cheese board.

Method:

- Peel and finely chop the onion.
- Heat the olive oil in a large saucepan over a low heat and cook the onion for 5 minutes.
- Peel and halve the carrots lengthways and then slice them.
- Deseed and finely chop the chilli.
- Add the carrots and chilli to the pan and cook for a couple of minutes.
- Add the tomato puree and cook for 1 minute.
- Rinse the lentils and drain and rinse the chickpeas and the kidney beans.
- Add the lentils, chickpeas and kidney beans along with the vegetable stock, chopped tomatoes and water.
- Bring to the boil, then turn down the heat and cover the pan, simmering for 30 minutes.
- Serve piping hot with some crusty bread on the side.

Ingredients: – serves 4–5

1 large onion

2 tbsp olive oil

3 carrots

1 red chilli

2 tbsp tomato puree

200g green lentils

1 x 400g can of chickpeas

1 x 400g can of kidney beans

500ml vegetable stock

1 x 400g can of chopped tomatoes

500ml water

SCRAMBLED EGGS

I would rate scrambled eggs up there with mashed potatoes and chicken soup as a comfort food. I have learned over the years that although they are quick to make they require your undivided attention. Scrambled eggs stuck and burnt to the bottom of the pan are not the scrubber's friend, so keep stirring! For breakfast, brunch or supper, scrambled egg served with wholemeal toast and supplemented with baked beans makes a nutritious and filling meal.

Method:

- Melt the butter in a saucepan over a medium heat.
- Meanwhile, whisk the eggs in a bowl with the milk, salt and pepper.
- When the butter is melted, add the egg and milk mixture.
- Use a wooden spoon to continuously mix the eggs as they scramble and do not allow any to stick to the bottom of the pan.
- Cook to your desired consistency (I tend to keep them on the wet side of moist, as they will continue to cook and dry when taken off the heat).
- Stir well and serve on hot buttered wholemeal toast with a garnish of chopped fresh chives or parsley.

Ingredients:

Small knob of butter per person

2 eggs per person

Splash of milk

Good pinch of salt and ground black pepper

Fresh parsley or chives to garnish

TIP: For a special breakfast use cream instead of milk.

OMELETTE

When you are at your wits' end and need to produce a quick meal, turn to the ultimate standby food, an omelette. They can be served plain or with any of your favourite fillings. Even adding just a teaspoon of dried herbs to an omelette will give it lots of flavour. *Suggested fillings*: **chopped cooked ham, chopped tomatoes, chopped onion, sweetcorn, sliced mushrooms, grated cheese, chopped bacon, a sprinkle of dried herbs, e.g. oregano, herbes de Provence.**

Method:

- Prepare the filling you intend to use by chopping it and frying or heating any of the fillings that may need a little bit of cooking, e.g. mushrooms, onion, sweetcorn, bacon. Cheese works best if it is grated.
- Heat the sunflower oil in a frying pan over a medium to high heat.
- Meanwhile, whisk the eggs in a bowl with a splash of milk and season with salt and white pepper.
- Tip the egg mixture into the frying pan and as the egg begins to solidify use a fish slice/ spatula to pull in the egg from the edge of the pan and allow any wet mixture to flow out to the edges of the pan. Cook for 1 minute.
- Scatter the toppings over the omelette and cook for a further 2 minutes.
- Use a spatula to fold one half of the omelette over the other and sandwich the filling in the middle.
- Press down and cook for 1 minute more.
- Garnish with fresh parsley or chives, and serve with a side salad, or, to make it even more substantial, with home-made potato wedges (see p. 39).

Ingredients:

2 tsp sunflower oil

2 eggs per person/omelette

Splash of milk per person

Ground sea salt flakes

Ground white pepper

Fresh parsley or chives to garnish

FRITTATA

Have a good rummage around your fridge and store cupboard and I am sure you will find plenty of ingredients to fill a frittata. A couple of stray mushrooms – perfect; a lonely wilting pepper – divine; a hardening chunk of cheese – reincarnate it with a grater to sprinkle over the frittata. This is a great way to use leftover cooked potatoes to very quickly rustle up a nutritious meal. I am suggesting adding rashers and mushrooms here, but you could substitute cooked ham for the rashers and maybe sliced red pepper instead of mushrooms. Traditionally frittatas are cooked first on the hob and then under the grill, whereas here I bung everything into a baking dish and cook it in the oven.

Method:

- Preheat the oven to 180°C/Gas Mark 6.
- Lightly grease an ovenproof casserole or baking dish with a little butter.
- Chop the rashers into bite-size pieces.
- Wash and slice the mushrooms.
- Heat the olive oil in a frying pan and fry the bacon and mushrooms for 4 minutes.
- Whisk the eggs in a bowl, then whisk in the sour cream and season with salt and pepper.
- Chop up the cooked potatoes into bite-size chunks and slice the spring onions, add them to the bacon and mushrooms, and cook for 2 minutes.
- Tip the contents of the pan into the casserole or baking dish and pour over the egg mixture.
- Bake for 15 minutes until the egg has risen slightly and set.
- Serve hot with a garnish of chopped fresh chives or parsley and a side of dressed salad leaves.

Ingredients: – serves 4–5

Butter to grease dish

8 rashers of bacon

10 button mushrooms

2 tbsp olive oil

8 eggs

50g sour cream

Ground salt (or flakes) and ground black pepper

4 leftover cooked potatoes

2 spring onions

Fresh parsley or chives to garnish

STUFFED BAKED POTATOES

A potato does not always have to be a side dish and with this recipe it gets to shine. I love the simplicity of bunging them into the oven and leaving them to do their thing. The essential ingredients are the potatoes, butter and cheese – everything else is flexible.

Method:

- Preheat the oven to 200°C/Gas Mark 7.
- Wash and scrub the potatoes, but leave the skin on and pat dry with a kitchen towel.
- Prick the potatoes all over with a fork and bake them in the oven directly on the rack for around 50–60 minutes until the middle is cooked and soft. You can test this by inserting a knife, which should slide in easily.
- Peel and crush the garlic.
- Melt the butter in a small saucepan or frying pan over a medium heat and gently cook the crushed garlic for 1 minute and set to one side.
- Chop the cooked ham or chicken into small pieces and set aside.
- Grate the cheese and set aside.
- Rinse and finely chop the chives or parsley if using.
- Cut the cooked potatoes in two and scoop the flesh out into a bowl, sprinkle in the dried or fresh herbs, pour in the melted butter and garlic, and mash well. Keep the skins for re-filling.
- Add the chopped chicken or ham, season with salt and pepper and mix well.
- Place the potato skins on a baking tray and fill with the potato mixture, top with the grated cheese and return to the hot oven for around 5 minutes until the cheese melts.
- Serve with a leafy salad or with a fried egg for a more substantial meal.

Ingredients: – serves 4

4 large potatoes

2 garlic cloves

75g unsalted butter

Cooked ham or chicken (approx. 100g)

50g cheddar cheese

Small handful of fresh chives or fresh parsley or 1 tsp of dried herbs such as herbes de Provence

Ground salt (or flakes) and ground black pepper

TIP: Try using a basil or tomato pesto mashed through the potatoes instead of the herbs.

CRISPY POTATO SKINS

These are better than any crisps I have ever tasted. When kids are absolutely *starving* and cannot wait until dinner is ready, this is a delicious filler to keep them going. An ideal time to make them is when you are making mashed potatoes for dinner and will be peeling potatoes anyway.

Method:

- Preheat the oven to 200˚C/Gas Mark 7.
- Wash, scrub and pat the potatoes dry with a kitchen towel.
- Peel the potatoes and place the peelings on a large baking tray.
- Drizzle over the olive oil and season with salt and pepper.
- Cook for 20–25 minutes until they are nice and crispy.
- Grate the cheddar cheese over the peelings and return to the oven for a further 3–5 minutes until the cheese has melted and is turning golden.
- Spice them up with a sprinkling of cayenne or chilli powder if you wish.

Ingredients: – serves 4–6

6 to 8 medium potatoes (1 to 2 per person)

3 tbsp olive oil

Ground sea salt and ground black pepper

50g cheddar cheese

Cayenne or chilli powder (optional)

POTATO WEDGES

Potato wedges are an indulgence food and a great alternative to chips. As they are cooked in their skins, you get the health benefits of the fibre even if they are soaking up the oil. You can cook these without spices if you prefer them plain, but sprinkling them with something like paprika or a mild chilli powder will enhance both their flavour and appearance.

Method:

- Preheat the oven to 200°C/Gas Mark 7.
- Wash and scrub the potatoes and pat dry with a kitchen towel.
- Cut each potato in half lengthways leaving the skin on and then slice each half into four wedges.
- Spread the wedges out onto two baking trays, drizzle generously with the olive oil, and sprinkle the spices on top.
- Season with salt and pepper.
- Cook for 30–35 minutes until crispy and golden brown, turning them over halfway through the cooking time. Cooking time will vary depending on the size of potatoes and wedges – test with a knife to check that they are tender in the middle.
- Serve with a portion of baked beans, a generous scattering of grated cheese and a side salad for a complete and simple meal.

Ingredients: – serves 4–6

6 to 8 medium potatoes (1 to 2 per person)

3 tbsp olive oil

Paprika or cayenne pepper or Cajun seasoning or chilli powder to sprinkle

Ground sea salt flakes and ground black pepper

TIP: Make them healthier by scattering over a good handful of finely chopped parsley.

QUESADILLAS

This tasty Mexican food sandwiches two tortillas together and can be filled with anything you like as long as it contains some grated cheese (*queso* is the Spanish for cheese) to meld it all together. Quesadillas are perfect for a Saturday afternoon spent watching a match on TV.

Method:

- Grate the cheese and peel and finely chop the red onion.
- Spread one side of each tortilla with the sun-dried tomato pesto or paste.
- Place 2 slices of ham on a tortilla and top with chopped red onion and grated cheese and sandwich together with a second tortilla.
- Heat a large non-stick frying pan over a medium heat and place a quesadilla on the pan pressing it down so that the heat will begin to toast the underside of the tortilla and penetrate through to melt the cheese.
- Turn it over after 1 or 2 minutes and press down to lightly toast the other side until the cheese has melted.
- Serve immediately.

Ingredients: – serves 6

200g cheddar cheese

1 small red onion (if you don't like raw onion leave it out)

8 large soft flour tortillas

Sun-dried tomato pesto or paste

8 slices of cooked ham

TIPS: Quesadillas are great served with guacamole and sour cream. Cold quesadillas are perfect for school lunchboxes.

SPAGHETTI WITH PESTO, BACON AND BROCCOLI

I love quick suppers and this is an all-time favourite in my house. The pesto and some of the cooking water forms the sauce in this dish, so for a pasta dish it is relatively light. Cooking the broccoli in the same water as the spaghetti gives the pasta great flavour and saves on the washing up.

Method:

- Fill up a large saucepan with boiling water and bring it back to the boil.
- Prepare the broccoli by giving it a quick rinse and breaking it up into florets and set aside.
- Peel and crush the garlic and set aside.
- Rinse and slice the cherry tomatoes in half and set aside.
- Cook the spaghetti in the boiling water for 6 minutes, while gently frying the rashers in a frying pan in 1 tablespoon of the olive oil.
- Occasionally stir the spaghetti so that it does not stick together.
- After 6 minutes, add the broccoli florets to the spaghetti and cook for a further 2 minutes.
- Meanwhile, add 1 tablespoon of olive oil to the rashers and add in the crushed garlic and halved cherry tomatoes.
- After a total cooking time of 8 minutes drain the spaghetti and broccoli, retaining about a half a cup of the cooking water.
- Roughly chop the rashers in the pan and then stir the rashers, garlic and cherry tomato mix into the spaghetti and broccoli.
- Stir in the pesto and enough of the reserved cooking water to moisten.
- Serve hot with some extra pesto and grated Parmesan.

Ingredients: – serves 5–6

400g broccoli (1 small head)

2 garlic cloves

300g cherry tomatoes

400g dried spaghetti

10 rashers (approx. 300g)

2 tbsp olive oil

3 tbsp basil pesto (see overleaf for
   home-made recipe)

Grated Parmesan cheese to garnish

HOME-MADE PESTO

Home-made pesto is something that I will quite happily lick off the spoon. I am all for the easy life and have no problem with buying the odd jar in the supermarket, but once you have made your own there is no comparison. It will lift pasta, sandwiches, salads, cheese and burgers, and is great as a dip.

Method:

- Lightly toast the pine nuts in a dry heated frying pan over a medium heat until they begin to take on a golden colour, then remove from the heat. (Watch them carefully as they burn easily.)
- Rinse and roughly chop the basil.
- Finely grate the Parmesan and peel and crush the garlic.
- Combine everything with the olive oil in a food processor or mini chopper, and blend until smooth.
- Store in a sterilised old jam jar in the fridge.

Ingredients: for 350ml of pesto

50g pine nuts

Large bunch of fresh basil
   leaves (25g)

50g Parmesan cheese

2 garlic cloves

200ml olive oil

TIP: This traditional pesto is made with basil and known as Pesto alla Genovese. While basil is distinctive and wonderfully fragrant, you can substitute it with other herbs such as coriander or even rocket. Feel free to play around with the type of nuts and hard cheese you use too; I've used roasted hazelnuts successfully and would imagine that walnuts would produce an interesting pesto also.

PASTA BAKE QUICK DISH

I never throw away leftover cooked pasta. Instead I keep the pasta drizzled with a little olive oil in a container in the fridge. Hungry children will eat it cold or you can give it a blast in the microwave with some tomato puree or pesto for an instant snack. This recipe resurrects cold cooked pasta with some cooked meat and grated cheese to produce a quick and complete meal.

Method:

- Preheat the oven to 200°C/Gas Mark 7.
- Break the broccoli or cauliflower into florets, briskly cook in a saucepan of boiling water for 2 minutes and drain.
- Place the cold cooked pasta in an ovenproof baking dish, sprinkle it with a little water, drizzle over a little olive oil and the mixed herbs, and mix well.
- Add the broccoli or cauliflower florets and the chopped cooked meat and mix well.
- Bake in the oven for 10 minutes.
- Mix well, then grate the cheese on top and bake for 5 minutes more until steam is rising from the pasta and the cheese has melted and the meat is heated through.
- Dry-fry the pine nuts in a small frying pan until they turn golden.
- Serve the pasta with some pesto mixed through and the pine nuts sprinkled on top.

Ingredients: – serves 4

400g broccoli or cauliflower florets

400g leftover cooked pasta

Olive oil to drizzle

2 tsp mixed herbs

250g cooked ham or chicken

100g grated cheddar cheese

50g pine nuts

Tomato or basil pesto to serve

TIP: An alternative that works equally well is to mix some tomato puree and water through the pasta before reheating and use salami slices instead of chicken or ham.

TIP: Home-made garlic bread can be made very easily by mashing some butter with a crushed clove of garlic and generously buttering a baguette or ciabatta with it and then grilling it until the garlic butter melts.

* If you are using cooked ham, it could be ham that you have left over from a cooked joint or slices of packed cooked ham. Frying it up with the olive oil and then adding crushed garlic will heat it up and enhance the colour and flavour.

PASTA CARBONARA

Having played around with a number of Carbonara recipes, some with cream, some with wine, and then pared them back and chopped and changed quantities, I eventually came up with this recipe which is simple and scrumptious. As I am not a huge fan of pasta, this is one meal that has surprised me by how much I enjoy it. The heat of the pasta cooks the eggs as you stir them in and the Parmesan forms a smooth sauce with a little of the cooking water. This meal can be on the table in 20 minutes.

Method:

- Boil a large saucepan full of water and once it is boiling put the pasta on to cook for 8 minutes.
- While the pasta is cooking, chop up the rashers or cooked ham and cook in a large frying pan with the olive oil for 5 minutes.
- Next, peel and crush the garlic cloves and add them to the meat to cook for 1 minute.
- Whisk the eggs in a bowl and grate in half of the Parmesan. Give this a good whisk together. Grate and reserve the other half of the Parmesan for later.
- When the pasta is cooked, drain it, reserving about a cupful of the cooking water.
- Take the frying pan with the cooked rashers off the heat. Add the cooked pasta to the rashers and garlic and then pour the Parmesan and egg mixture over this with enough of the cooking water to moisten it and mix well. The heat of the pasta will cook the egg as you stir it through the pasta.
- Season with freshly ground black pepper.
- Serve with the remaining grated Parmesan sprinkled on top, garnished with freshly chopped parsley and some garlic bread on the side.

Ingredients: – serves 4–5

400g dried spaghetti or any pasta

10–12 rashers or a packet of 10 slices of cooked ham* (approx. 300g)

1 tbsp olive oil

2 garlic cloves

3 eggs

100g Parmesan

Black pepper

Small handful of fresh parsley to garnish

49

CREAMY CHILLI CHICKEN

I love the simplicity of using crème fraiche to quickly make a sauce for this zingy fresh-tasting dish. Full of crunchy vegetables that are briskly cooked, this highly nutritious, yet creamily comforting dish is quick and easy to prepare.

Method:

- Heat the olive oil in a large frying pan over a medium heat and brown the chicken on one side for 4 minutes.
- Meanwhile, peel and crush the garlic, deseed and finely chop the chilli and slice the red pepper.
- Turn the chicken breasts over and slice them lengthways into three or four strips to speed up the cooking on the second side for 2 minutes.
- Push the chicken to the sides of the pan, add the garlic, chilli and red pepper to the middle of the pan and cook for 1 minute.
- Peel, halve and finely slice the red onion.
- Chop the broccoli into florets and roughly chop the coriander.
- Add the broccoli, red onion and baby sweetcorn to the pan and cook for 2 minutes.
- Use a fine grater or a zester to zest the rind of the lemon. Add it to the pan with the juice of half the lemon.
- Add the cashew nuts and chopped coriander and mix well.
- Stir in the crème fraiche, heat through and serve with boiled baby potatoes or boiled rice.

Ingredients: – serves 4–5

1 tbsp olive oil

4 skinless chicken breasts

1 garlic clove

1 red chilli

1 red pepper

1 medium red onion

½ head of broccoli (approx. 200g)

Small bunch of fresh coriander

Handful of whole baby sweetcorn

1 lemon

Handful of cashew nuts

200g crème fraiche

CREAMY PESTO CHICKEN

As I write about this dish I can almost taste it. Fragrant, heady fresh basil deepens the flavour of the pesto and the cherry tomatoes ooze with bursting sweetness. The creamy sauce clings to every mouthful of the chicken to utterly satisfy.

Method:

- Heat the olive oil in a large frying pan or casserole pot over a medium to high heat.
- Fry the chicken on one side for 4 minutes.
- Peel, roughly chop and add the onion.
- Turn each chicken breast over and slice into three or four strips lengthways to speed up the cooking; cook for a further 2 minutes.
- Cut the cherry tomatoes in half, add to the pan and cook for 2 minutes.
- Add the pesto and crème fraiche and heat through, adding some water to bring the sauce to a consistency of your liking.
- Serve with pasta or a baked potato and a generous sprinkling of fresh basil leaves.

Ingredients: – serves 4–5

1 tbsp olive oil

4 skinless chicken breasts

1 large onion

300g cherry tomatoes

2 tbsp basil pesto

200g crème fraiche

Small bunch of fresh basil to garnish

LEMON AND CORIANDER CHICKEN

Scouring the pages for something low fat, yet filling and tasty? Then this is it. The addition of lemon zest and lemon juice lends this lovely, light dish cleansing properties. It's perfect for when you are feeling virtuous and kids don't seem to notice that they are wolfing down a super healthy dish. While chickpeas are high in protein, they are also high in fibre and starch, so you don't have to accompany this with rice, etc.

Method:

- Cut the chicken into bite-size chunks.
- Peel and thinly slice the shallots.
- Heat the olive oil in a frying pan and fry the chicken pieces with the shallots over a medium heat for about 5 minutes.
- Zest the lemon rind and add it to the chicken with the ground coriander and ground cumin and cook for 1 minute.
- Strain and rinse the chickpeas and add to the chicken along with the chicken stock. Bring to the boil, then reduce to a simmer and cover with a lid for 10 minutes.
- Cut the lemon in two and squeeze over all the lemon juice before serving with a scattering of fresh coriander leaves.

Ingredients: – serves 4–5

4 skinless chicken breasts

2 large shallots

1 tbsp olive oil

1 lemon

1 tsp ground coriander

1 tsp ground cumin

1 x 400g can of chickpeas

200ml chicken stock

Fresh coriander to garnish

TIP: Though perfect on its own, you can serve this with wholegrain rice and a dollop of low fat natural yoghurt to make it more substantial.

CHICKEN KIEV

Some days I just want to eat something that is finger-licking tasty, filling and comforting. Oozing with garlic butter, this dish is the opposite of virtuous. The herbed butter renders the chicken internally moist and the crunchy breadcrumb coating results in a great texture combination.

Method:

- Preheat the oven to 190°C/Gas Mark 6.
- Prepare the butter filling by crushing the garlic cloves and mashing them with the butter, Dijon mustard and finely chopped parsley.
- Beat the egg and milk together in a bowl wide enough to dip a chicken fillet into.
- Place the breadcrumbs on a large plate.
- Assemble the chicken Kievs by cutting a deep slit into one side of the chicken breast and filling it with a quarter of the garlic butter.
- Secure each slit side of the chicken breasts with a cocktail stick or skewer.
- Heat the olive oil in a large frying pan over a medium to high heat.
- Dip each chicken breast into the egg mixture and then coat in the breadcrumbs and fry for 2 minutes on each side to brown.
- Finish cooking the chicken breasts on a baking tray in the heated oven for 20 minutes until cooked through.
- Remove the cocktail sticks before serving with a leafy green salad and coleslaw (see p. 214) or potato wedges (see p. 39) and a garnish of parsley.

Ingredients: – serves 4

2 garlic cloves

100g unsalted butter

1 tsp Dijon mustard

Handful of fresh parsley or 2 tsp dried parsley

1 egg

1 tbsp milk

100g breadcrumbs (3 slices of wholegrain bread blitzed)

4 skinless chicken breasts

Cocktail sticks or skewers to secure

4 tbsp olive oil

TIP: To make breadcrumbs use a mini chopper to blitz a few slices of wholegrain bread in seconds.

CHICKEN NUGGETS

Home-made chicken nuggets are great finger food for a kid's party. As you will be using the oven anyway you could easily add some baked potatoes or potato wedges. I like to dip the nuggets into egg, then flour, then egg, then breadcrumbs to ensure that plenty of the seasoned flour coats the chicken pieces. Your fingers are going to get very messy so consider roping in a small child if there is one available – they will think it is great fun.

Method:

- Preheat the oven to 200°C/Gas Mark 7.
- Cut each chicken breast into eight even-sized nuggets.
- Mix the flour with the cumin and coriander and place in a shallow bowl or plate for dipping the chicken into.
- Beat the eggs in a bowl and put the breadcrumbs into another bowl for dipping.
- Coat the chicken pieces by dipping them into the egg, then into the seasoned flour, into the egg again and then rolling in the breadcrumbs.
- Heat two baking trays with 1 tablespoon of olive oil drizzled on each in the oven for 1 minute.
- Place the nuggets on the heated baking trays and cook in the hot oven for 15–20 minutes. Turn once in the middle of cooking.
- As the pieces are small, they should cook through easily, but test one by cutting through to the middle before serving.
- Serve hot with some ketchup and mayonnaise or barbecue sauce.

Ingredients: – serves 4–5

4 skinless chicken breasts

3 tbsp plain flour

2 tsp ground cumin

2 tsp ground coriander

2 eggs

125g breadcrumbs

2 tbsp olive oil

TIP: Increase the nutritional value of your breadcrumbs by whizzing up three or four slices of wholegrain bread with a little freshly chopped parsley. As well as being healthier, using wholegrain bread will give a better colour and crunchier texture to the crumbs.

59

CHICKEN AND BACON CASSEROLE

Using chicken pieces with the skin left on increases the flavour of this dish and adding rashers gives you that classic chicken and ham combination so it's almost like eating a soupy Sunday roast. This is another dish that I would consider comfort food and perfect for a cold day.

Method:

- Preheat the oven to 180°C/Gas Mark 6.
- Heat the olive oil in an ovenproof casserole pot on the hob over a medium to high heat and lightly brown the chicken pieces for 5 minutes.
- Peel and chop the onion into chunks and chop the rashers into bite-size pieces.
- Push the chicken to the side of the pot and add the onion and rashers to cook for 5 minutes.
- Peel and chop the carrots and set aside.
- Add the flour and herbs to the pot and mix with a wooden spoon to cook for 1 minute stirring it into the juices.
- Gradually add in the chicken stock and chopped carrots and bring to the boil.
- Put a lid on the casserole pot and transfer it to the oven to cook for 45–50 minutes.
- Deliciously comforting served with mashed potatoes.

Ingredients: – serves 5–6

2 tbsp olive oil

4–6 pieces of chicken (800g–1kg with skin on)

1 medium onion

4 rashers

4 large carrots

1 tbsp flour

1 tsp herbes de Provence

500ml chicken stock

TIP: The easiest way to cut raw rashers is with kitchen scissors.

CHICKEN, TOMATO AND RED PEPPER CASSEROLE

The red pepper and tomatoes bring a Mediterranean vibe to this casserole. There is plenty of liquid so it is best to serve it in bowls with crusty bread to mop up the juices.

Method:

- Preheat the oven to 180°C/Gas Mark 6.
- Heat the olive oil in an ovenproof casserole pot over the hob on a medium to high heat and brown the chicken pieces on all sides for 5 minutes. (Depending on the size of the pieces and your pot you may need to do this in batches.)
- Meanwhile, peel and slice the onions, crush the garlic and slice the red pepper.
- Push the chicken to the side of the pot and lower the heat.
- Add the sliced onions and cook for 3 minutes.
- Add the sliced red pepper and crushed garlic and cook for 1 minute.
- Peel and chop the carrots and set aside.
- Add the flour and mix it into the juices with a wooden spoon to create a paste.
- Gradually add in the chicken stock, the chopped tomatoes and carrots, and bring to the boil.
- Take the pot off the heat and transfer it to the oven.
- Cook in the oven with a lid on for 45–50 minutes.
- Great served with crusty bread or boiled baby potatoes.

Ingredients: – serves 5–6

2 tbsp olive oil

4–6 pieces of chicken (800g–1kg with skin on)

2 medium onions

2 garlic cloves

1 red pepper

4 large carrots

2 tbsp flour

250ml chicken stock

2 x 400g cans of chopped tomatoes

TIP: Any leftovers will make tasty soup reheated for lunch the next day or can be frozen to be used as a pasta sauce.

TIP: This chicken, leek and mushroom filling is great in vol-au-vent pastry cases too.

CHICKEN, LEEK AND MUSHROOM PIE

Pastry is incredibly filling so this pie is sure to satisfy the biggest of appetites. The pastry crust canopies succulent chicken and leeks enveloped in a rich mushroom sauce. Shortcrust pastry can be bought ready made and is usually stored in the freezer section of the supermarket, though some do keep it in the chilled cabinet too, which saves you the trouble of having to thaw it out.

Method:

- Prepare the pastry and leave it to rest (or defrost if shop bought).
- Preheat the oven to 180°C/Gas Mark 6.
- Prepare the leek by cutting off the root and discarding any darker outer leaves. Slice the leek in half lengthways and rinse, then finely slice the leek and rinse again in a colander (as the leek grows in layers, dirt can get trapped in between).
- Melt the butter and olive oil together in a large frying pan over a low heat. Add the leek to the oil and butter and leave to soften while you chop the chicken into bite-size chunks.
- Add the chicken to the leek with the thyme and turn up the heat to medium and cook for 5 minutes. Meanwhile, wash and slice the mushrooms.
- Push the chicken out to the sides of the pan and cook the mushrooms for 2 minutes.
- Add the flour, mix well and cook for 1 minute. Gradually add the milk/water mix and stir well to thicken the sauce. Simmer for 15 minutes.
- Transfer the chicken and leek mixture to a large ovenproof baking dish and cover the top with the pastry. Brush over the pastry with the beaten egg and milk and prick the top of the pastry with a fork or score with a knife to vent it in a few places.
- Bake in the hot oven until the pastry is golden brown – this should take around 25 to 30 minutes. Serve with boiled wholegrain rice.

Ingredients: – serves 4–5

1 quantity shortcrust pastry (see p. 160 to make your own, or buy frozen and thaw out)

1 leek

50g unsalted butter

1 tbsp olive oil

4 skinless chicken breasts

2 tsp thyme

8 large button mushrooms

2 tbsp flour

300ml milk mixed with 100ml water

1 egg and a splash of milk for egg wash on pastry

Crunchy and succulent, sweetcorn is one of my favourite vegetables. I have been known to eat a whole can of it simply heated in a saucepan with a knob of butter and a generous sprinkling of black pepper. If you are not a big fan of sweetcorn, try this recipe with canned garden peas instead. Comforting mashed potatoes are smoothed on top making this a chickeny alternative to shepherd's pie.

CHICKEN, LEEK AND SWEETCORN BAKE

Method:

- Preheat the oven to 180°C/Gas Mark 6.
- Peel the potatoes, cut them in two and bring to the boil in a saucepan of water for 20 minutes until soft enough to mash.
- Prepare the leek by cutting off the root and discarding any darker outer leaves. Slice the leek in half lengthways and rinse under a cold tap. Finely slice the leek and rinse again in a colander (as the leek grows in layers, dirt can get trapped in between) and set aside.
- Chop the chicken into bite-size chunks.
- Heat the sunflower oil in a large frying pan over a medium heat and add the washed sliced leek and the chopped chicken. Cook for 10 minutes.
- Add the crushed garlic and cook for 1 minute.
- Add the chicken stock and stir in the crème fraiche.
- Take the pan off the heat and place the chicken mix in a casserole or baking dish.
- Drain and add the sweetcorn and mix well.
- Strain and mash the potatoes with the butter and enough milk to make them easy to spread over the chicken mix.
- Dot the potatoes here and there with a little more butter.
- Cook in the preheated oven for 15–20 minutes until the potatoes are beginning to brown and the sauce is bubbling.
- Serve with a garnish of fresh chives or parsley.

Ingredients: – serves 5

10 medium-sized potatoes

1 leek

4 skinless chicken breasts

1 tbsp sunflower oil

1 garlic clove

500ml low salt chicken stock

100g crème fraiche

1 x 340g can of sweetcorn

50g unsalted butter

A little milk

Butter to dot on potatoes

Fresh chives or parsley to garnish

SWEET AND SOUR CHICKEN

We used to be addicts of a certain Uncle's jar of sweet and sour sauce until I experimented with a number of recipes and devised this one. Everyday tomato ketchup, malt vinegar, brown sugar and pineapple juice are used to create a tangy dish balanced with just the right amount of sweetness.

Method:

- Peel and chop the carrot into julienne (thumb-length, skinny cut) pieces.
- Peel and chop the onion into chunks, crush the garlic, deseed and finely chop the red chilli, slice the spring onions and set aside.
- Chop the chicken into bite-size pieces.
- Heat the olive oil in a wok or large frying pan over a high heat and stir-fry the chicken pieces for 3 minutes.
- Add the chopped onion to the chicken and cook for 2 minutes, using a wooden spoon or spatula to move the chicken and onion and stop them from sticking or burning as they cook.
- Slice the red pepper and add it to the chicken with the crushed garlic, chopped chilli and carrot batons and stir well.
- Drain the pineapple rings, reserving the juice, and chop them into chunks.
- Add the chopped pineapple, tomato ketchup, malt vinegar and the sugar and stir well to coat everything.
- Add the spring onions, 3 tablespoons of pineapple juice and 3 tablespoons of water and continue to cook until all the ingredients are heated through.
- Serve with boiled or steamed rice.

Ingredients: – serves 5

1 large (or 2 medium) carrots

1 medium onion

2 garlic cloves

1 red chilli

2 or 3 spring onions

4 skinless chicken breasts

1 tbsp olive oil

1 red pepper

1 small can of pineapple rings –
220g undrained in own juice
(4 rings)

8 tbsp tomato ketchup

3 tbsp malt vinegar

2 tbsp muscovado or dark brown
sugar

ROAST CHICKEN AND ROAST POTATOES WITH HERB STUFFING AND GRAVY

What could be more perfect for Sunday dinner than a roast chicken with roast potatoes, gravy and stuffing? This is a dinner to sit down to, indulge and enjoy. I have listed a conservative number of potatoes here, as two should be enough per person, but are there ever enough roast potatoes when there is all that tasty gravy to be mopped up? Any stuck-on bits are fought over and prised from the pan in my house, and I'm sure I'm not the only one who sticks her hand in the fridge for a leftover cold one, sprinkled with a little salt. Delicious.

Ingredients: – serves 6

1 large chicken (approx. 2kg)

1 lemon

Olive oil to drizzle

Sea salt

12 medium potatoes (at least)

For the stuffing:

1 large onion

100g unsalted butter

400g breadcrumbs

1 tbsp dried parsley

1 tbsp dried thyme

For the gravy:

2 tbsp flour

500ml chicken stock

Method:

The stuffing – make up the stuffing and leave it to cool before you put the chicken on to cook.

- Peel and finely chop the onion.
- Melt the butter in a saucepan over a low heat and soften the onion in the pan with a lid on for 5–10 minutes.
- Turn off the heat and stir in the breadcrumbs, parsley and thyme.
- Transfer the mixture to a baking dish and leave to cool.

The chicken

- Preheat the oven to 190°C/Gas Mark 6.
- Cut the lemon in half and place both pieces in the cavity of the chicken.
- Place the chicken in a roasting tray, drizzle olive oil over it, season with some crumbled sea salt flakes and put it in the oven.
- Work out the cooking time of your chicken, which will vary by weight (20 minutes per 450g + 20 minutes extra).

Cooking the roast potatoes

- Peel and parboil the potatoes (cut into roughly equal-sized pieces) for 10 minutes.
- Drain the potatoes and rattle them in the saucepan to bash the outside for a crunchier roastie.
- Roast the parboiled potatoes for 1 hour around the side of the chicken, coated with the chicken juices – and some extra olive oil towards the end of the chicken's cooking time.

Cooking the stuffing

- Cover the cooled stuffing with tinfoil and cook for 45 minutes towards the end of the cooking time for the chicken. Toss the stuffing with a fork halfway through the cooking time so that it cooks evenly.

Making the gravy

- Remove the chicken and potatoes from the roasting tin and place the tin on the hob over a low heat.
- Scrape up all the juices and mix with the flour to make a paste and cook for 2 minutes.
- Gradually add in the chicken stock, stirring continuously, bringing it to the boil, then reduce to simmer for 5 minutes.
- Note: If you think there is an excessive amount of fat and juices, pour some off. Generally, I use 1 tablespoon of flour to 2 tablespoons of fat and juices to 400/500ml stock, and double this for a larger meal, e.g. Christmas Dinner. For a thicker gravy, use more flour. If you want to be healthier, place some ice cubes in the juices: this should cause the fat to solidify, so you can easily skim some off.
- Serve the chicken, stuffing, potatoes and gravy with some cooked frozen peas or a tray of roasted carrots and parsnips.

TIP: If all the potatoes do not fit around the chicken use a separate tray and spoon some of the chicken juices and a good drizzle of olive oil over them. Any leftover stuffing can be frozen in sandwich bags to use for school sandwiches. Leftover chicken can be used to make soup.

MUSHROOM AND PINE NUT STUFFING

I love stuffing and for me nothing beats a mouthful of stuffing with Brussels sprouts and gravy at Christmas Dinner. Truthfully it does not even need the gravy – I will quite happily put my hand in the fridge and scoop out a handful of stuffing to enjoy all by itself.

Method:

- Preheat the oven to 190°C/Gas Mark 6.
- Peel and finely chop the onion.
- Melt the butter in a saucepan over a low heat.
- Add the onion and put the lid on the saucepan to soften and sweat the onion for 5–10 minutes.
- Meanwhile, wash and chop the mushrooms into small pieces and set aside.
- Dry-fry the pine nuts (no oil) in a hot frying pan for 1 minute, tossing them until they turn golden. (Watch carefully as they burn easily.) Take the frying pan off the heat and set aside.
- Add the chopped mushrooms to the onions, raise the heat to medium and cook for 2 minutes.
- Take the saucepan off the heat and stir in the breadcrumbs, thyme and pine nuts.
- Transfer the mixture to a baking dish and leave to cool.
- Bake for around 40–50 minutes in a hot oven. Toss the stuffing with a fork halfway through cooking so that it cooks evenly.
- Serve hot with a chicken or turkey dinner and some delicious gravy.

Ingredients:

1 small onion

100g unsalted butter

250g mushrooms

50g pine nuts

200g breadcrumbs

1 tsp dried thyme

RATATOUILLE ONE-POT CHICKEN

I was very surprised when I first made this dish that the kids actually tried the aubergine and courgette without protest, as they are not vegetables I use that often. The kids are fans of the movie *Ratatouille* and probably fancied themselves as the restaurant critic character in the film!

Method:

- Preheat the oven to 190°C/Gas Mark 6.
- Crush the garlic.
- Chop the aubergine into 2cm cubes and set aside.
- Heat 1 tablespoon of the olive oil in a large casserole dish on the hob over a medium heat and gently fry up the crushed garlic for 1 minute.
- Add the dried parsley and cubed aubergine and mix well. Lower the heat and leave to soften for 10 minutes, stirring occasionally.
- Meanwhile, roughly chop the tomato and slice the courgette, red pepper and onion into rings.
- Turn off the heat and layer the vegetables over the softened aubergine in the casserole dish.
- Dollop the tomato puree on top and add 125ml of water to the pan.
- Place the chicken breasts on top of everything and drizzle over the other tablespoon of olive oil.
- Season with salt and black pepper.
- Cook in the oven for 45 minutes (turn the chicken over after 20 minutes and gently press it down into the vegetables to keep it moist).
- Serve with boiled basmati rice.

Ingredients: – serves 6

3 garlic cloves

1 aubergine

2 tbsp olive oil

2 tsp dried parsley

1 tomato

1 courgette

1 red pepper

1 medium onion

1 x 150g can or tube of tomato puree

125ml water

5 skinless chicken breasts

Sea salt and ground pepper

PIRI PIRI CHICKEN

The chicken is cooked directly on an open rack in the oven with a baking tray on the shelf beneath to catch the dripping fat and marinade juices. If you're feeling indulgent then put a tray of potato wedges on the second shelf to cook in this fat and juices – bad, bad, bad but very good! The chicken needs to be marinated overnight or for at least three hours before cooking for maximum flavour.

To marinate

- Peel and roughly chop the onion, ginger and garlic and then blitz these in a food processor with the olive oil, piri piri sauce, lemon juice, salt and pepper.
- Place the chicken pieces in a bowl and cover with the marinade. Cover and leave in the fridge for 3 hours or overnight if possible.

Method:

- Preheat the oven to 200°C/Gas Mark 7.
- Place the marinated chicken pieces directly on a rack/oven shelf and sprinkle with paprika.
- Cook the chicken pieces for 20 minutes with a baking tray on the oven shelf underneath to catch the dripping fat.
- Turn the chicken over, sprinkle again with paprika and cook for a further 10 to 20 minutes until nicely browned and cooked through.
- Great served with potato wedges cooked in the marinade and oils dripping from the chicken as it cooks.

Ingredients: – serves 5–6

1 small onion

3cm thumb-width piece of ginger

3 garlic cloves

50ml olive oil

50ml piri piri sauce (or Tabasco or Worcester sauce)

Juice of half a lemon

1 tsp ground sea salt

Half tsp ground black pepper

6 chicken pieces (with skin on)

Paprika to season and colour

BEEF STEW

Beef stew takes over two hours to cook, so it is not a recipe for when you are in a hurry. If I am going to the bother of making a stew, I like to make double this quantity and use the leftovers to make Cornish pasties the following day. Marinate the beef in a covered bowl in the fridge overnight or for a few hours before cooking as this will make the meat more tender. If you forget or do not have time to marinate it, just leave out this step.

To marinate:

- Crush the garlic cloves and mix with 4 tablespoons of olive oil and soy or Worcester sauce.
- Pour marinade over the beef and leave in a covered bowl in the fridge overnight or for 4 to 6 hours before using.

Method:

- Preheat the oven to 150˚C/Gas Mark 3.
- Peel and chop the onions and carrots and set aside.
- Put the flour on a large plate and sprinkle with salt and pepper.
- Heat 1 tablespoon of olive oil in an ovenproof casserole dish over a medium heat on the hob.
- Toss the beef in the flour and then quickly brown the meat in the casserole dish.
- Turn off the heat, add the onions, carrots and the hot stock, and mix well.
- Transfer the covered casserole dish to the oven and cook for 1 hour.
- Peel and chop the potatoes in half and peel and chop the parsnips, then add to the stew, pressing the parsnips and then the potatoes well down into the stew.
- Turn the heat up to 170˚C/Gas Mark 5 and cook for 1 more hour.
- Serve with a garnish of chopped parsley and some crusty bread to mop up the juices.

Ingredients: – serves 6–8

2 garlic cloves for marinade

5 tbsp olive oil (or 1 tbsp if not marinating)

2 tbsp soy or Worcester sauce for marinade

1kg stewing beef pieces, e.g. shin

2 medium onions

4 large carrots

4 tbsp plain flour

Sea salt and ground pepper

1 litre hot beef stock

10 medium potatoes

2 parsnips

CORNISH PASTY

Make the most of stew leftovers by turning them into deliciously filling Cornish pasties. This is a dish that now has protected status and only those made in Cornwall can be sold as Cornish pasties. Traditionally they would be made with an uncooked filling of beef, potatoes and onion. Using already cooked stew lessens the cooking time.

Method:

- As shortcrust pastry needs to rest in the fridge for a half an hour before you use it, make it up ahead of time.
- Preheat the oven to 200°C/Gas Mark 7.
- Roll the pastry into a large rectangular shape a bit larger than a baking tray.
- You will need to divide the pastry into six pieces to make six individual pasties. I generally do this by cutting four squares of pastry from the first rolling and then re-rolling the excess pastry to divide into two more squares.
- Drain most of the liquid from the stew and reserve to reheat separately and serve with the pasties when cooked.
- Chop the cold stew into bite-size pieces.
- Spoon a heap of stew just off-centre on each pastry square.
- Beat the egg and the milk together and use the egg wash to wet the edges of the pastry.
- Fold the longer side of pastry over the top to form a parcel and pinch or roll the edges of the pastry together with your fingers to seal it. You can press the edges with a fork to seal it firmly.
- Brush over the top of each pasty with the egg wash and score a couple of small vents into the top with a knife.
- Cook on baking trays in the preheated oven for 30 minutes until the pastry is golden brown and steam is rising from the pastry vents to ensure that the stew is thoroughly reheated.
- Reheat the leftover stew gravy separately in a saucepan and serve with the pasties.

Ingredients: – serves 6

1 quantity savoury shortcrust pastry (see p. 160)

Cold cooked stew – approx. 750g weight

1 egg beaten with a splash of milk

TIP: You can cheat and buy the shortcrust pastry.

MOROCCAN BEEF STEW

A warmly spiced alternative to a regular stew, this is perfect when you want something comforting in the winter months. I make it up in a large quantity and, like a regular stew, any leftover Moroccan beef would be a great filling for a pastry-wrapped pasty.

Method:

- Preheat the oven to 150°C/Gas Mark 3.
- Peel and finely chop the onion.
- Heat the olive oil in a large casserole pot and gently fry the onion for 5 minutes over a low heat.
- Raise the heat to medium, push the onion to the sides of the pot, add the beef, and brown for 2 minutes.
- Peel and crush the garlic and finely chop or grate the ginger and then add it to the centre of the pot to cook for 1 minute.
- Add the ground cinnamon and ground coriander and cook for 1 minute.
- Add the tomato puree, canned tomatoes, water and honey and mix well.
- Cook the casserole in the oven for 2 hours with a lid on. Check it after an hour and if there are any signs of it drying out, add some more water.
- Serve hot with buttery mashed potatoes or boiled rice, with a side of green beans or mange tout.

Ingredients: – serves 6–8

1 medium onion

1 tbsp olive oil

1kg stewing beef pieces, e.g. shin

3 garlic cloves

3cm thumb-width piece of ginger

1 tsp ground cinnamon

1 tsp ground coriander

1 tbsp tomato puree

2 x 400g cans of chopped tomatoes

100ml water

2 tbsp runny honey

HOME-MADE BEEFBURGERS

Making your own burgers means you know exactly what's in them and that they are free of sulphur dioxide, which is an additive that is often used in commercial burgers and is a known allergen. It takes seconds to make your own breadcrumbs and using wholegrain bread will make it healthier.

Method:

- Lightly beat the egg in a bowl.
- Peel and finely chop the onion and crush the garlic.
- Place the mince in a large bowl and add the onion, garlic, breadcrumbs, herbs and beaten egg and season with salt and pepper. Mix thoroughly with a fork.
- Shape the mixture into six balls and flatten into burger shapes with your hands.
- Heat the olive oil in a frying pan over a medium to high heat and cook the burgers for about 5 minutes on the first side until nicely browned.
- Turn the burgers over and lower the heat slightly to medium and cook for a further 15–20 minutes, turning the burgers once more halfway through cooking and pressing down with a spatula to encourage heat to penetrate through the burger.
- Test that the burger is thoroughly cooked by cutting through to the centre with a knife. There should be no pink meat and the juices should run clear.*
- Serve in a toasted burger bun or ciabatta with some potato wedges and salad.

Ingredients: – serves 6

1 egg

1 small onion

2 garlic cloves

500g round steak mince

100g breadcrumbs (3 slices bread blitzed – wholegrain if possible)

2 tsp herbes de Provence, oregano, or basil

Sea salt and ground pepper

2 tbsp olive oil

TIP: Change the position of the burgers on the pan halfway through cooking as those at the centre will tend to cook more quickly than those at the edge of the pan.

*It is extremely important to test that the burgers are cooked through to the middle as bacteria that may exist on the surface of a piece of meat can be minced into it and needs enough heat to kill it.

SPAGHETTI MEATBALLS

I think kids love meatballs because they are fun-sized, manageable food. They love spaghetti because they love to mess with their food, twirl it around the fork and suck up the strands, which makes spaghetti meatballs a kid-friendly combination. Something else that they love is to get stuck into the preparation of the meatballs, squishing the meat, herbs and breadcrumbs in between their fingers, and then rolling them into little balls. It is perfectly safe for them to do this as long as they do not taste any raw mixture and give their hands a good wash both before and afterwards.

Method:

- Preheat the oven to 190°C/Gas Mark 6.
- Lightly beat the egg in a bowl and set aside.
- Place the minced meat in a large mixing bowl.
- Peel and finely chop the onion and crush the garlic and add them to the minced meat along with the herbs, breadcrumbs and beaten egg. Use a fork to combine the mixture and season with salt and pepper.
- Pour the chopped tomatoes, tomato puree and water into an ovenproof casserole or baking dish, and mix well with a wooden spoon.
- Use your hands to shape the meat into golf-ball-sized meatballs (around 20) and arrange in the tomato mixture in the casserole dish.
- Cook in the oven for 30–35 minutes until the meatballs are cooked through.
- When the meatballs are almost ready, boil a large saucepan of water and cook the spaghetti for 8 minutes.
- Test that the meatballs are thoroughly cooked by cutting through to the centre of one with a knife. There should be no pink meat and the juices should run clear.
- Serve the spaghetti with the meatballs and sauce on top, with a garnish of fresh basil leaves.

Ingredients: – serves 5–6

1 egg

500g round steak mince

1 small onion

2 garlic cloves

2 tsp herbes de Provence, oregano, or basil

100g breadcrumbs (3 slices bread blitzed – wholegrain if possible)

Sea salt and ground pepper

1 x 400g can of chopped tomatoes

2 tbsp tomato puree

150ml water

400g spaghetti

Fresh basil leaves to garnish

SHEPHERD'S PIE

Shepherd's pie can be made with minced beef or lamb, although for purists it should really be made with lamb, while cottage pie is made with mince. It is a meal that is worth all the trouble for the pleasure of eating. When the peeling and chopping is all done, you do not even need to use a knife and fork to eat it, a spoon will do just as well. I sometimes top it with a little grated cheese and flash it under the grill to make it extra special. Using grated carrots in the recipe is a subtle way of getting more vegetables into children. It is also a great way of stretching the meal if you have some unexpected company.

Method:

- Preheat the oven to 190°C/Gas Mark 6.
- Peel the potatoes. Fill a saucepan of water and put them on to boil.
- Heat the olive oil in a large saucepan and brown the mince over a medium heat.
- Meanwhile, peel and grate the carrots and set aside.
- Add the mixed herbs to the browned mince and mix through.
- Add the tomato puree to the meat and cook for 1 minute, then add the grated carrots.
- When the potatoes are cooked, mash them with butter.
- Make up the 500ml of vegetable stock in a jug of boiling water, add the frozen peas and leave to stand for 1 minute.
- Pour the peas and stock into the bottom of a casserole dish. Top with the meat and carrot mix and then the mashed potatoes. Put a few dots of butter here and there on top of the potatoes. Cook in the oven for 30 minutes.
- Serve hot with a garnish of chopped parsley.

Ingredients: – serves 5–6

10 to 12 medium-sized potatoes

1 tbsp olive oil

500g round steak mince (or lamb mince)

3 medium carrots

1 tsp mixed herbs

2 tbsp tomato puree

Butter for mashing and topping potatoes

500ml hot vegetable stock (from cube is fine)

300g frozen peas

TIP: You can add some Worchester sauce and grated celery for extra flavour.

CHILLI CON CARNE

Chilli con carne is very filling and is a lovely warming dish. I would rate the heat of this one as medium. If you prefer your chilli with a bit more kick then add another teaspoon of chilli powder.

Method:

- Heat the olive oil in a large deep frying pan or saucepan and brown the mince over a medium to high heat until the juices run clear.
- While the mince is browning, finely chop the onions, dice the pepper into small pieces and crush the garlic.
- Push the browned mince to the side of the pan, add the chopped onion and red pepper to the centre, and cook on a medium heat for 5 minutes.
- Push the onion and pepper towards the sides, add the garlic, chilli powder, paprika and cumin, and cook for 1 minute.
- Add the tomato puree, sugar, oregano, beef stock and chopped tomatoes and mix well.
- Bring to the boil then reduce the heat to a simmer for 20 minutes, stirring occasionally.
- Strain, rinse and add the kidney beans and return to the boil.
- Reduce the heat again and simmer for 5 more minutes.
- Great served with a baked potato and a dollop of sour cream with a garnish of chopped fresh parsley or chives.

Ingredients: – serves 6

1 tbsp olive oil

500g round steak mince

2 medium onions

1 red pepper

2 garlic cloves

1 tsp hot chilli powder

1 tsp paprika

1 tsp cumin

2 tbsp tomato puree

1 tsp white sugar

1 tsp oregano

500ml beef stock

1 x 400g can of chopped tomatoes

1 x 400g can of kidney beans

Fresh parsley or chives to garnish

TIP: Canned kidney beans come pre-cooked and are more convenient than dried beans which would need to be soaked and cooked.

BOLOGNESE SAUCE

This meat-based sauce is perfect with spaghetti or any pasta and serves as a base for lasagne. The traditional recipe varies and some versions use celery, pancetta, milk and not as much tomato as I do, but this is how we like it. This dish requires slow cooking to maximise flavour. The alcohol in the wine will evaporate off in cooking, but if you would prefer you can use beef stock instead.

Method:

- Peel and finely chop the onions and peel and dice the carrots.
- Heat the olive oil in a large saucepan over a medium heat and cook the onions and carrots for 10 minutes until softened.
- Crush the garlic and add to the saucepan to cook for 1 minute.
- Push the carrots and onions to the side of the pan, turn up the heat and add the mince. Cook for 10 minutes breaking it up with a spatula as it cooks.
- Add the tomato puree and the mixed herbs and mix well.
- Add the plum tomatoes, red wine, black pepper, salt and bay leaf.
- Bring to the boil and then reduce the heat to simmer for 2 hours until the sauce is well reduced and thickened. Stir occasionally as it cooks and use the back of a wooden spoon to squash and break down the plum tomatoes.
- Delicious served with any type of pasta and some crusty garlic bread to mop up the juices. Discard the bay leaf before serving.

Ingredients: – serves 5–6

2 medium onions

3 medium carrots

3 tbsp olive oil

4 garlic cloves

500g minced beef

4 tbsp tomato puree

1 tsp mixed herbs (mix of marjoram, basil, oregano and thyme)

2 x 400g cans of plum tomatoes

300ml red wine

1 tsp ground black pepper

2 tsp salt

1 bay leaf

TIP: For a quick version leave out the carrots and bay leaf and simmer for 30 minutes instead of 2 hours.

LASAGNE

A basic white sauce is known as Béchamel and becomes Mornay sauce when cheese is added to it. Mornay sauce is used as the creamy layer that pairs up with Bolognese sauce in a traditional lasagne. In this recipe, I do not quite go to the lengths that it takes to produce an authentic Béchamel sauce, infusing onion and cloves in scalded milk, but it is close enough! The cheese used is traditionally a mixture of Gruyère, Emmental or Parmesan, but I use white cheddar.

Method:

- Preheat the oven to 190°C/Gas Mark 6.
- *To make the white sauce*: melt the butter in a saucepan over a medium heat and stir in the flour with a wooden spoon to make a paste (roux) and cook for 2 minutes.
- Add the mustard and mix well, raise the heat and then slowly add the milk, stirring continuously to form a smooth sauce.
- Thicken for a few minutes and then add 125g of grated cheese, stirring well as it melts to combine into a smooth sauce.
- Build up the lasagne layers in a baking dish, beginning with a layer of meat sauce and then a layer of lasagne sheets. The next layer will be meat sauce followed by white sauce and then lasagne sheets. The last layer (depending on the size of your dish) will be meat sauce followed by a final layer of white sauce.
- Finish by sprinkling some grated cheddar cheese on top of the white sauce.
- Bake in the oven for 40 minutes.
- Serve hot with a leafy green salad.

Ingredients: – serves 5–6

1 quantity Bolognese sauce
  (see previous recipe)
25g unsalted butter (approx.
  1 heaped tbsp)
1 tbsp flour
1 tsp English mustard
400ml milk
150g cheddar cheese (25g of this is
  for grating on top)
9 to 10 fresh or dried lasagne
  sheets

TIP: It doesn't really matter how you assemble the layers of your lasagne as long as both sides of the pasta sheets are in contact with either Bolognese sauce or white sauce for moisture and that you finish with a layer of white sauce which will turn golden when sprinkled with cheese.

BEEF AND MUSHROOM STIR-FRY

Finally, a super quick beef dish for when you are in a hurry. The steaks are very thinly cut so they will cook in minutes.

Method:

- Thinly slice the steak into strips and set aside.
- Wash and slice the mushrooms.
- Rinse and break the broccoli into florets and set aside.
- Peel and crush the garlic and finely chop or grate the ginger and set aside.
- Heat the oil in a hot wok or large frying pan.
- Quickly fry the steak strips until browned and push to the edges of the pan.
- Add the mushrooms and cook for 2 minutes.
- Push the mushrooms to the side, add the ginger, garlic and broccoli, and cook for 1 minute.
- Mix in with the steak and mushrooms.
- Drizzle over the honey and stir well, then add in the soy sauce.
- Mix the cornflour and cold water together and add to the pan.
- Continue to cook until the sauce is thoroughly heated and serve on a bed of noodles.

Ingredients: – serves 4–5

4 thin or 2 thick striploin steaks (400g)

150g mushrooms

300g broccoli

1 garlic clove

3cm thumb-width piece of ginger

1 tbsp groundnut or sesame oil

2 tbsp runny honey

2 tbsp rich soy sauce

2 tsp cornflour

200ml cold water

TIP: Add quicker cooking vegetables such as baby sweetcorn and sugar snap peas for added nutrition and crunch.

95

TIP:
Oomph up your mashed potatoes by adding some cream cheese and wholegrain mustard if you like it.

BANGERS AND MASH WITH RED ONION GRAVY

What is not to love about bangers and mash? This is the ultimate comfort food, loved by adults and kids alike. Butcher-style sausages are incredibly meaty and you can get some great varieties that have herbs and even mustard added. The best sausage I have ever tasted was made in front of my eyes by Declan O'Flynn of 'O'Flynn's Gourmet Sausage Company' in the world-renowned English Market in Cork city. Named the 'Cork Boi' it's made with pork mince, onion, thyme, 'secret seasoning', breadcrumbs and Murphy's Irish Stout.

Method:

- Peel the potatoes and cut to a uniform size, then place in a saucepan, cover with boiling water and bring to the boil. Cook for 20–30 minutes until cooked through.
- While the potatoes are cooking, peel and chop the onions in half and then into thin slices.
- Heat 1 tablespoon of the olive oil in a small saucepan over a low heat and add the onions. Leave to soften with the lid on for 15 minutes.
- Prick the sausages on all sides with a fork so they do not burst their skins.
- Heat 1 tablespoon of olive oil in a frying pan over a medium heat and add the sausages. Turn the sausages occasionally until brown on all sides.
- When the onions have softened, add the brown sugar and balsamic vinegar, then turn the heat up for 2 minutes to allow it to bubble and begin to evaporate. Add the stock to the onions, bring it to the boil then reduce to simmer for 10 minutes.
- When the potatoes are cooked, drain off the water and mash well with the butter and enough milk to make a creamy consistency.
- Serve the sausages and mash with some easy-to-cook vegetables, such as cabbage or broccoli and red onion gravy spooned on top.

Ingredients: – serves 4

8–10 large potatoes

2 medium red onions

2 tbsp olive oil

8 butcher-style sausages

1 tbsp dark brown sugar

5 tbsp balsamic vinegar

500ml beef stock

50g unsalted butter for mashing potatoes

Splash of milk for mashing potatoes

BUTCHER'S SAUSAGE HOTPOT

Hotpot is another meal that is up there on the comfort food scale. Besides having to peel and slice the potatoes and an onion, there is very little preparation involved in making this meal.

Method:

- Preheat the oven to 190°C/Gas Mark 6.
- Peel and thinly slice the potatoes.
- Put the potatoes in a saucepan of boiling water, bring to the boil and cook for 4–5 minutes (they should be getting tender but not soft or they will disintegrate), drain them and set aside.
- Peel and slice the red onion into rings.
- Heat the olive oil in a large frying pan over a medium to high heat and begin to brown the sausages.
- Add the onion rings to the frying pan.
- Make up the beef stock in a large jug and add the mixed herbs and the frozen peas to the jug of hot stock.
- Once the sausages are browned on all sides add the stock/pea mix and stir well to scrape up any meat residue on the bottom of the pan.
- Transfer the sausages, etc. into a baking or casserole dish and arrange the potato slices on top.
- Dot the potatoes here and there with some butter.
- Bake in the oven for 15–20 minutes.
- Serve hot with a garnish of parsley.

Ingredients: – serves 4

8–10 large potatoes

1 small red onion

1 tbsp olive oil

8 butcher-style sausages

500ml hot beef stock (cube is fine)

2 tsp dried mixed herbs

400g frozen peas

Butter for dotting onto potatoes

Fresh parsley to garnish

TIP: No time for sausage hotpot? Then do not forget hotdogs. When I was working on editing this book I was perched up on the kitchen counter one Saturday lunchtime after my twin boys' soccer match and squeezing in an hour before bringing one of my daughters, Ellie, to bag packing for the Athletics Club. The Gravy Man (my husband) made a lunch of fat butcher sausages in crispy fresh baguettes with gently fried onions and a dollop of ketchup. Yum.

GOLDEN SYRUP BAKED HAM

The tradition of soaking and boiling a ham before baking it has prevailed from times when hams were heavily salted to preserve them, but with today's refrigeration and modern techniques there are ham cuts such as dry cured loin of bacon that can be baked straight in the oven without the need for soaking first. Leftover baked ham is perfect for ham sandwiches.

Method:

- Preheat the oven to 180°C/Gas Mark 6.
- Place the ham on a baking tray and use a knife to score diagonal lines into the fat, criss-crossing them.
- Push a clove into the centre of each section of the fat.
- Drizzle the ham with olive oil and sprinkle with some sea salt flakes crumbled with your fingers.
- Bake the ham in the oven for 1 hour then take it out and drizzle the golden syrup over the top of the fat. Pour some water into the baking tray, just enough to cover the base – this will stop the dripping golden syrup from burning and will create a lovely sauce to pour over the ham.
- Return the ham to the oven for 20 minutes.
- Serve with mashed potatoes, cabbage and parsley sauce (see p. 113).

Ingredients: – serves 4

800g–1kg dry cured loin of bacon or unsmoked back bacon joint or rib joint

Whole cloves

1 tbsp olive oil

Sea-salt flakes

2 tbsp golden syrup

A little water

PORK CHOPS IN CREAMY HONEY AND MUSTARD SAUCE

This is a lick the plate clean comfort food dish. Pork can be a dry meat, particularly in the form of chops if they are just fried and allowed to shrink and toughen up. This dish browns the chops for flavour and then immerses them in a sweet creamy sauce to tenderise and moisturise them.

Method:

- Preheat the oven to 190°C/Gas Mark 6.
- Heat the olive oil in a large frying pan over a medium to high heat and fry the chops on each side for a couple of minutes, until beginning to brown.
- Meanwhile, peel and finely chop the onion.
- Remove the chops from the pan and place on a baking tray in the oven to continue cooking while you make the sauce.
- Lower the heat in the frying pan and cook the onion for 5 minutes until they begin to soften.
- Add the flour and mix well to scrape up any meat residue from the bottom of the pan. Turn the heat up to medium and cook for 1 minute.
- Raise the heat to high and gradually add the chicken stock and then the apple juice, stirring continuously.
- Add the honey and mustard and stir well.
- Remove the chops from the oven and turn it off. Transfer the chops back into the pan, lower the heat to a gentle simmer and cook for 10 minutes.
- Just before serving add in the cream and raise the heat to heat through.
- Serve with equally comforting mashed potatoes and maybe some green beans, broccoli or cabbage.

Ingredients: – serves 4

1 tbsp olive oil

4 pork chops

1 medium onion

1 tbsp flour

250ml chicken stock

250ml apple juice

1 tbsp creamed honey

2 tbsp wholegrain mustard

150ml carton of double cream

PAN-FRIED FISH WITH CARROT AND PARSNIP MASH

Fish is probably the ultimate fast food and a fillet of fish can be cooked in less than 5 minutes. When I was growing up, fish was compulsory eating in practically every household in Ireland on a Friday. The side dish of carrots and parsnips is a combination that my mom regularly served up.

Method:

- Peel and chop the carrots and parsnip.
- Put the carrots in a saucepan of boiling water, bring back to the boil and cook until tender – around 15 to 20 minutes.
- When the carrots have been cooking for 10 minutes prepare to cook the fish.
- Put the milk in a bowl and 2 tbsp flour on a separate plate. Season the flour with salt and pepper.
- Heat the olive oil in a pan over a high medium heat, dip each piece of fish in the milk, then coat with the flour, and put on the pan to cook skin-side down. Turn the fish over after 2 minutes.
- Meanwhile, add the parsnip to the carrots.
- Cook the fish for 2 minutes on the second side and take the pan off the heat.
- Drain the carrots and parsnip and mash together with the butter, seasoning with salt and pepper.
- Serve the fish with the carrot and parsnip mash garnished with chopped fresh parsley and lemon wedges, or to make this meal more substantial serve it with mashed potatoes and parsley sauce (see p. 113).

Ingredients: – serves 4

4 large carrots

1 large parsnip

75ml milk

2 tbsp flour

Sea salt and ground pepper

1 tbsp olive oil

4 fillets of white fish: cod/whiting/ sea bass, etc.

Unsalted butter for mashing vegetables (approx. 25g = 1 heaped tbsp)

1 lemon and fresh parsley to serve

TIP: Any leftover carrot and parsnip mash is great mixed with some onion softened in butter with ground coriander, and then fried up as a sort of veggie cake the next day.

FISH PIE

I keep forgetting how great fish pie is and each time I make it I vow to do so more regularly. Packed with onion, parsley, carrots, parsnips, broccoli and fish, this is a well-balanced, nutritious meal. You will need to make up a quantity of basic white parsley sauce. Try the butcher counter of your local supermarket for a medley of fish pieces – mine does a great one.

Method:

- Preheat the oven to 190°C/Gas Mark 6.
- Peel and boil the potatoes in a saucepan of water for 20 to 25 minutes until cooked.
- While the potatoes are cooking, make up the white sauce and set aside (see p. 113).
- Peel and chop the carrots and parsnip and break up the broccoli into florets and set aside. Boil the carrots in a saucepan of water for 5 minutes.
- Toss the fish pieces in a bowl with the flour seasoned with sea salt and black pepper.
- While the potatoes and carrots are cooking, heat the olive oil in a medium to hot pan and put the fish pieces on the pan to cook for 4 minutes.
- Meanwhile, add the parsnip to the partially cooked carrots.
- Take the fish off the heat and place it in an ovenproof casserole dish.
- Add the broccoli to the carrots and parsnip to cook for 1 minute, then drain.
- Put the carrots, parsnip and broccoli into the casserole dish with the fish and pour the white sauce on top.
- Drain and mash the potatoes with 100ml milk and 50g butter and spread over the fish mix.
- Bake in the oven for 20 minutes.
- Serve with wedges of lemon and a garnish of chopped fresh parsley.

Ingredients: – serves 5–6

10 medium-sized potatoes

1 quantity white parsley sauce

2 large carrots

1 parsnip

Half head of broccoli (approx. 200g)

600g mixed fish pieces

2 tbsp flour

Sea salt and ground pepper

1 tbsp olive oil

100ml milk for mashing potatoes

50g unsalted butter for mashing potatoes

1 lemon to serve and fresh parsley to garnish

THAI FISHCAKES

This is a lovely, fresh-tasting dish with the zing of lime. Full of fish and potatoes they are great served with simply dressed salad leaves with an Asian salad dressing (see p. 215).

Method:

- Peel, boil and mash the potatoes if you do not have any leftovers to use up.
- Poach the salmon in a saucepan of hot water for about 5 minutes, strain into a colander and flake into a bowl.
- Leave the salmon to cool for a few minutes. (There should be roughly the same amount of salmon as potato.)
- Meanwhile, rinse and chop the spring onions, peel and crush the garlic, zest and juice the lime, deseed and roughly chop the chilli and combine all of these in a food processor.
- Mix the flaked salmon, mashed potatoes and spring onion mixture in a bowl and then shape into small cakes with your hands.
- Heat the olive oil in a frying pan over a medium to high heat.
- Beat the egg in a bowl and put the flour on a plate.
- Dip each fishcake into the egg and then into the flour to lightly coat it. Fry on the first side until they are beginning to brown, turn the fishcakes over and lower the heat to cook for a further 3–4 minutes until cooked through.
- Serve with lemon wedges and some dressed salad leaves.

Ingredients: – serves 5–6

Leftover cooked mashed potato or
   3 potatoes boiled and mashed

4 salmon darnes (approx.
   480g–500g)

2 spring onions

2 garlic cloves

1 lime

1 red chilli

2 tbsp olive oil

1 egg

3 tbsp plain flour

1 lemon to serve

SALMON IN SOY SAUCE

Eating this salmon dish always makes me feel healthy. The salmon needs to be marinated for an hour or two, or ideally overnight, to infuse with the flavour of the marinade. Other than that, this is a super quick dish to prepare.

To marinate:

- Peel and crush the garlic and grate the ginger.
- Deseed and finely chop the red chilli and slice the spring onions.
- Combine the garlic, ginger and chilli with the spring onions and soy sauce to make a marinade and pour it over the salmon. Leave to marinate (refrigerated) for 1 or 2 hours, or ideally overnight, covered with cling film.

Method:

- Heat the olive oil in a large frying pan on a medium to high heat.
- Add the salmon pieces skin-side down and cook for 2 minutes, reserving the marinade sauce.
- Turn the salmon over and cook for a further 2 minutes, then add the marinade sauce and heat through for 1 minute before serving.
- Great as a light lunch served with Asian dressed salad (see p. 215) or green beans.

Ingredients: – serves 4

3 garlic cloves

3cm thumb-width piece of ginger

1 red chilli

2 spring onions

50ml dark or rich soy sauce

4 salmon darnes (approx. 480–500g)

1 tbsp olive oil

SALMON AND BASIL ONE POT

Salmon, cherry tomatoes and baby potatoes all are roasted together making this a very easy one-pot dish. To increase the vegetable intake, serve this with some green beans, which only take a couple of minutes to cook in boiling water. Salmon can be quite expensive, so I would consider this dish to be dinner-party worthy, maybe spruced up a little with some sliced black olives.

Method:

- Preheat the oven to 200°C/Gas Mark 7.
- Cut the baby potatoes in half (skins on) and toss in a large roasting pan or dish with 1 tablespoon of the olive oil.
- Put the potatoes on to roast in the oven for 20 minutes.
- Toss the potatoes and make room for the salmon darnes and the cherry tomatoes still on the vine.
- Drizzle 1 tablespoon of the olive oil over the salmon and tomatoes, and drizzle the balsamic vinegar over the tomatoes.
- Cook for a further 10–15 minutes.
- Serve the salmon with a garnish of fresh basil leaves and wedges of lemon.

Ingredients: – serves 4

1kg washed baby potatoes

2 tbsp olive oil

4 salmon darnes (approx. 480–500g)

1 punnet of cherry tomatoes (on the vine if possible)

1 tbsp balsamic vinegar

Small bunch of fresh basil

Lemon to serve

TIP: Great with a dollop of sour cream and a side of green beans.

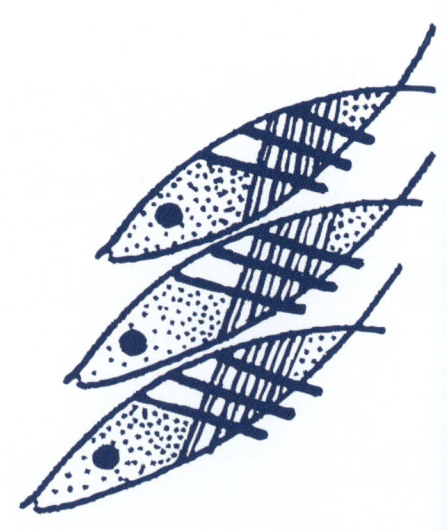

BASIC WHITE PARSLEY SAUCE

This sauce works really well with fish and ham/bacon. It is also great over cooked cauliflower with grated cheese sprinkled on top and melted under the grill.

Ingredients:

1 small onion

Small handful of flat-leaf parsley

50g unsalted butter

2 tbsp flour

400ml milk

Method:

- Peel and finely chop the onion.
- Rinse and finely chop the parsley.
- Melt the butter in a saucepan, add the onion and soften for 5 minutes over a low heat, then stir in the parsley.
- Add the flour and use a wooden spoon to mix into a paste with the butter and onion.
- Turn up the heat and gradually add the milk, stirring continuously, and bring to the boil.
- Take off the heat immediately and serve.

LIME WHITE SAUCE

This sauce is a little bit more special than its poor parsley relation and is all the more fancy for the addition of cream. It's great with pan-fried salmon or sea bass. The method for making it is more or less the same as the basic white parsley sauce without the onion.

Ingredients:

1 lime

50g unsalted butter

1 tbsp flour

1 tsp ground coriander

250ml cream

Method:

- Zest and then juice half the lime.
- Melt the butter in a saucepan over a low heat, add the flour and use a wooden spoon to mix into a paste.
- Add the ground coriander and lime zest and mix well.
- Turn up the heat to a high medium and add the lime juice.
- Keep stirring and slowly add the cream.
- Bring to a gentle boil.
- Take off the heat immediately and serve.

RED THAI CHICKEN CURRY

I did not discover Thai food until I was in my twenties and in Amsterdam, and it has been a favourite of mine ever since. My local supermarket is wonderfully progressive and they sometimes offer a basket filled with the ingredients for making a Thai curry paste. To make your own red Thai curry paste see the next recipe.

Method:

- Make up the red Thai curry paste if using home-made.
- Peel and chop the onion in half and then into thin slices.
- Heat the sunflower oil in a large saucepan over a low heat and soften the onion for 5 minutes.
- Meanwhile, chop the chicken breasts into bite-size chunks.
- Add the curry paste to the onion, mix well and cook for 1 minute.
- Raise the heat to medium and add the chicken chunks and stir to coat them with the paste.
- Add the brown sugar, fish sauce, lime zest and coconut milk and stir well.
- Bring to the boil then reduce the heat and simmer for 15 minutes.
- Serve with freshly chopped coriander leaves and boiled basmati rice.

Ingredients: – serves 4–5

2½ tbsp home-made red Thai curry paste (see overleaf) or 1 tbsp red Thai curry paste from a jar

1 medium onion

1 tbsp sunflower oil

4 skinless chicken breasts

1 tsp brown sugar

1 tbsp fish sauce (nam pla)

Zest of 1 lime

1 x 400ml can of coconut milk

Bunch of fresh coriander

TIP: Use low-fat coconut milk in the curry if you are watching the fat content.

RED THAI CURRY PASTE

Deliciously aromatic, this will keep in the fridge for a week and makes enough for 2 Thai curries. Lemon grass makes for a more authentic Thai-style curry, but if you cannot get hold of it just leave it out and the recipe will work just as well.

Method:

- Deseed and roughly chop the chillies and red pepper.
- Roughly chop the lemon grass, fresh coriander and ginger and crush the garlic.
- Peel and finely chop the shallots and zest the lime.
- Whiz all the prepared ingredients with the black pepper and ground coriander in a food processor to create a paste.

Ingredients:

3 red chillies

½ red pepper

1 stalk of lemon grass

Small handful of fresh coriander

3cm thumb-width piece of ginger

2 garlic cloves

3 shallots

Zest of 1 lime

1 tsp ground black pepper

1 tsp ground coriander

TIP: Store in a sterilised jar in the fridge for a week to ten days.

INDIAN CHICKEN CURRY

The inclusion of garam masala in this curry gives it an Indian orientation. Garam masala is not a hot spice in the sense of burning your mouth, but it is hot in terms of warming or heating from the inside. It is a blend of numerous spices and the spices that it contains vary from region to region in India, but usually include cinnamon, cloves, peppercorns, black cardamom, cumin and coriander. The chilli powder on the other hand will bring hot heat to the table – truth be known my preference is for 3 teaspoons of hot chilli powder, but my testers found that to be too much so I have pared it back to 2. If you prefer your curry mild, reduce the hot chilli powder to 1 teaspoon.

Method:

- Peel and finely chop the shallots or onions.
- Heat the olive oil in a large deep frying pan or saucepan over a low heat and fry the shallots or onions for 5 minutes until softened.
- Chop the chicken into bite-size pieces.
- Peel and crush the garlic.
- Peel and grate or finely chop the ginger.
- Turn the heat up to medium, add the chopped chicken, crushed garlic and finely chopped ginger, and cook for 1 minute.
- Add the hot chilli powder, turmeric and garam masala, and mix well to coat the chicken. Cook for 2 minutes.
- Add the coconut milk and vegetable stock, bring to the boil then reduce the heat and simmer for 20 minutes.
- Serve with boiled rice and some naan bread or chapattis* to mop up the juices.

Ingredients: – serves 4–5

8–10 small shallots or 3 small onions

1 tbsp olive oil

4 skinless chicken breasts

2 garlic cloves

3cm thumb-width piece of ginger

2 tsp hot chilli powder (or 1 if you prefer mild)

1 tsp ground turmeric

4 tsp garam masala

1 x 400ml can of coconut milk

250ml vegetable stock

* Chapattis are Indian flat breads made using wholewheat flour and water, sometimes with the addition of cumin seeds, coriander and garlic.

CHICKEN TIKKA MASALA

To stay true to the Indian way of cooking tikkas (pieces), the chicken is cooked separately to the sauce. Do not be put off by the long list of ingredients, as they are mostly spices. There are two stages to this dish: 1) marinating and 2) cooking. Marinating the chicken overnight maximises flavour and results in more tender, succulent chicken.

To marinate:

- Crush the garlic and grate the ginger.
- Deseed and roughly chop the chillies.
- Place the garlic, ginger, turmeric, chillies, paprika, cumin, ground coriander and garam masala into a food processor and blitz to make a paste.
- Mix half of the paste in a large bowl with the yoghurt. Reserve the other half of the paste for the cooking stage.
- Cut the chicken into chunks and marinate in the paste mixture (covered with cling film and refrigerated) either overnight or for at least 1 hour before cooking.

Ingredients: – serves 5–6

6 garlic cloves

6cm thumb-width piece of ginger

1 tsp turmeric

2 red chillies

1 tbsp paprika

2 tsp ground cumin

2 tsp ground coriander

2 tbsp garam masala

200g natural yoghurt

4 skinless chicken breasts

2 medium onions

25g unsalted butter (approx. 1 heaped tbsp)

2 tbsp tomato puree

400ml water

100ml double cream

Small bunch of fresh coriander

Method:

- Preheat the oven to 190°C/Gas Mark 6.
- Peel, halve and thinly slice the onions.
- Melt the butter in a pan and gently cook the sliced onions, over a low heat, mixed with the remaining half of the spice paste for 15 minutes.
- Add the tomato puree and 400ml of water to the sauce and simmer for 10 minutes.
- Heat a large dry frying pan or griddle pan on a high heat and brown the marinated chicken tikkas for about 2 minutes on each side, then place on a baking tray in the oven to finish cooking. Doing this ensures that the chicken pieces remain moist.
- To make the sauce add the double cream to the cooked onions mixture and just bring to the boil, then take it off the heat. Add the cooked chicken pieces to the sauce.
- Serve with boiled rice and a garnish of roughly chopped fresh coriander.

LAMB CURRY

Here's another long list of ingredients; however, for this curry there is no paste-making or marinating, just a bit of chopping and then the curry is left to simmer for an hour and a half to tenderise the lamb.

Method:

- Wash and roughly chop the tomatoes.
- Peel, halve and finely chop the shallots.
- Peel and crush the garlic and deseed and finely chop the chillies.
- Heat 1 tablespoon of olive oil in a large saucepan or casserole dish over a medium to high heat and brown the lamb in batches for a few minutes, removing it to a plate when it is browned.
- Add 1 tablespoon of olive oil to the pan, lower the heat and cook the shallots, garlic and chillies for 5 minutes.
- Add the turmeric, garam masala, cumin and mild chilli powder and cook for 1 minute.
- Add the flour and mix for 1 minute, then add in the tomatoes and coconut milk.
- Put the lamb back in along with its juices and the chicken stock and mix well.
- Simmer gently over a low heat with the lid on for 1½ hours, stirring occasionally.
- Stir in the yoghurt just before serving with some rice and naan bread.

Ingredients: – serves 6–8

6 large tomatoes

4 shallots

3 garlic cloves

2 green chillies (use red if green are not available)

2 tbsp olive oil

1kg lamb pieces

1 tbsp ground turmeric

1½ tbsp garam masala

1½ tbsp ground cumin

1 tbsp mild chilli powder

1 tbsp plain flour

1 x 400ml can of coconut milk

250ml chicken stock

200g plain yoghurt

EASY HOME-MADE PIZZA

When you do not want to bother with yeast, this scone-based pizza dough is quick and easy to make and rolled out thinly will fill two baking trays to make two large pizzas. My favourite topping combination is goat's cheese, basil pesto and red onion. *Suggested toppings:* crispy bacon pieces, sliced mushrooms, jalapeno peppers, sliced peppers, sliced olives, pieces of cooked chicken or ham, red onion, sweetcorn, pesto, mozzarella, grated cheddar, dried herbs.

Method:

- Preheat the oven to 200°C/Gas Mark 7.
- Lightly grease two baking trays with a little butter.
- Sift the flour into a bowl, add the cubed butter and crumble together with your fingertips until the mixture resembles breadcrumbs.
- Add a good splash of water to the flour and butter and combine first using a fork, then use your hands to bring it together to form a ball of dough. If you find that the dough is very sticky add a little more flour.
- Use some flour to lightly dust the worktop and the dough and gently knead it using the heel of your hand.
- Cut the dough in half and use some more flour to dust a rolling pin and the dough, then begin to roll each piece out. (It will not look like enough to cover a baking tray but keep rolling and it will.)
- After every couple of rolls lift the pastry and give it a half twist around to stop it from sticking to the table, and use more flour to dust if required.
- Continue to roll into a very thin rectangular shape the size of the baking tray.
- Place the pizza base onto the baking trays and spread it with the tomato puree or tomato pesto.
- Assemble the toppings and bake in the oven for 10 to 15 minutes.

Ingredients: – serves 6

Butter to grease tins

250g self-raising flour

50g unsalted butter, cubed

A little water

Extra flour for kneading and rolling

140g tube or 150g can of tomato puree or sun-dried tomato pesto

PROPER PIZZA

An authentic pizza base requires the use of yeast, a bit of waiting and a bit of kneading. The process can be speeded up a bit by using fast-action yeast and with the aid of a dough hook. The resulting pizza dough produces a light, crispy base. I have made dough once doing the kneading by hand and never again! Instead, I let the dough hook attachment on my 'Kenwood Major' do the work while I have a coffee.

Ingredients: – serves 6

Pizza dough:

375g strong flour or '00' Tipo flour

1 tsp dried oregano

7g sachet of fast-action bread yeast

1 tsp olive oil

250ml tepid water

Extra flour for kneading and rolling

Pizza Base Sauce:

1 medium onion

1 garlic clove

1 small handful of fresh basil leaves or 1 tsp dried oregano or basil

1 tbsp olive oil

1 x 400g can of chopped tomatoes

Dough

- Sift the flour into the electric mixing bowl and sprinkle in the oregano.
- Make a well in the centre and pour in the yeast followed by the olive oil and tepid water.
- Using the dough hook attachment mix the pizza dough on a low setting for 10 minutes.
- Cover the bowl with cling film and leave to rest for 1 hour.

Sauce:

- Peel, halve and finely chop the onion and crush the garlic.
- Chop the fresh basil if using.
- Heat the olive oil in a small saucepan over a medium heat.
- Soften the chopped onion in the saucepan for 5 minutes.
- Add the garlic and cook for 1 minute.
- Add the chopped tomatoes and herbs and simmer for 5 to 10 minutes.
- The longer it is cooked the thicker and richer the sauce.
- Blend the sauce to a smooth consistency.

Pizza

- Preheat the oven to 200°C/Gas Mark 7.
- Heat two baking trays in the oven – as the dough will be lightly floured it should not stick.
- Turn out the pizza dough and lightly dust it with flour and knead it for 1–2 minutes.
- Divide the dough in half and then knead, stretch and roll each half to the size of a baking tray.
- Top with the tomato sauce and whatever other toppings you wish and bake for 15 to 20 minutes until crisp.

COMPLETELY CHEATING PITTA PIZZAS

These are quick and easy to make, and are an ideal snack food. I sometimes wrap them in parchment paper for school lunches.

Method:

- Preheat the grill.
- Sprinkle the pitta with water and heat in the toaster for a couple of minutes so it puffs up.
- Slice each pitta bread open into two halves.
- Spread each half with a thin layer of the sun-dried tomato paste or red pesto.
- Top with whatever you fancy and grated cheddar cheese, sprinkle with oregano and grill until the cheese has melted.
- Serve with a scattering of chopped fresh herbs if you have them or black pepper.

Ingredients:

Round pitta breads – 1 per person

Sun-dried tomato paste or red pesto

Cheddar cheese

1 tsp oregano

Toppings: chorizo, salami, red onion, cooked ham, cooked chicken

BAKING DAY

- Bread, Scones and Teabrack
- Muffins, Cupcakes and Icing
- Cookies and Biscuits
- Pastry and Fruit Pies
- Brownies and Cakes
- Puddings and Pavlova

BAKING DAY

Of all the cooking that I do, baking is probably the most satisfying, enjoyable and rewarding. The thrill of opening the oven to discover that whatever it contains has actually risen and now looks scrumptious never fades.

What I have also discovered is that baking is incredibly easy, particularly if you invest in an electric mixer. Believe me, I am not one for kneading and when it comes to making dough or bread I'll happily leave the machine to do the hard stuff. Luckily my mother gave me her mixer, which has attachments for whisking and beating, as well as a dough hook.

Besides being easy, baking is also incredibly quick. You can have a batch of chocolate cupcakes ready to devour in half an hour. Kids are fascinated by baking and love to help, and it is a great way to occupy them on a rainy Saturday afternoon. At Christmas time, if you have kids who are old enough to read, they will be more than capable of putting together a batch of home-made biscuits and will do a beautiful job decorating them as presents. There is no need for you to be hands on in this type of baking. Give them the recipe, a scales, turn on the oven and, supervising from a distance, let them loose.

'Baking Day' presents simple recipes for baking both old-fashioned fare, such as brown bread, scones and Victoria sponge cakes, and more modern foods like chocolate chip cookies, brownies and sun-dried tomato bread.

Baking makes me smile and brings huge satisfaction in return for very little effort.

Note: When baking buns and cakes try to leave the butter and eggs out of the fridge for an hour or two beforehand. It will be easier to cream the butter and there will be less chance of the eggs curdling.

I use parchment paper a lot when baking to line trays and cake tins. If you are using it be sure that you use parchment paper and not greaseproof paper which will stick to the food.

BROWN BREAD

The recipe for this brown bread came home from the kids' school. It is simple, healthy and moist, and does not fall apart when you cut into it. When I asked their teacher Síle where she got it, she told me that it came from Folláin. Folláin is a company based in Cúil Aodha, County Cork, that produces delicious fresh fruit preserves, marmalades, jams, relishes, salsas and chutneys made with 100% natural ingredients. The name is the Irish for wholesome. The only change I have made to the original recipe is to increase the buttermilk a little.

Method:

- Preheat the oven to 170°C/Gas Mark 5 and lightly grease a 2lb loaf tin with a little butter.
- Mix all the dry ingredients together in a bowl (two flours, salt, bread soda, dark brown sugar).
- Make a well in the centre and add the sunflower oil and buttermilk.
- Mix well with a wooden spoon and pour the mixture into the greased loaf tin.
- Bake for 40–45 minutes.
- Turn out from the tin to cool on a wire rack. The bread should sound hollow when you lightly tap the base.
- Delicious served simply with butter and jam.

Ingredients:

225g wholemeal flour

225g plain flour

1 tsp salt

1 tsp bread soda

1 tsp dark brown sugar

2 tbsp sunflower oil

300ml buttermilk

Butter to grease the tin

SEMI-SUN-DRIED CHERRY TOMATO BREAD

I do not bake breads requiring yeast and rising time very often; however, I do find this one well worth the effort. I discovered semi-sun-dried cherry tomatoes as an own-brand product labelled 'Antipasto' in my local supermarket. Semi-sun-dried cherry tomatoes are sweeter and more moist than regular semi-sun-dried tomatoes, but the regular kind will do fine if you cannot find them. Let the dough hook on the mixing machine do all the hard work for kneading this bread.

Method:

- Sift the strong flour into the bowl of the electric mixer.
- Finely chop the semi-sun-dried cherry tomatoes and add them in. Add the thyme, rosemary, salt and the tomato puree.
- Make a well in the centre and add in the yeast and then the water. Using the dough hook on the electric mixer leave it to mix for 6 minutes on a low speed. The consistency of the dough will be quite moist, sticky yet loose.
- Cover the mixer bowl with cling film and leave to rise for 1 hour – your kitchen is generally a warm enough place for dough to rise.
- Preheat the oven to 200°C/Gas Mark 7.
- Use a pastry brush to grease a baking tray with the olive oil and pour the dough into a fat, oval shape.
- Brush the dough with olive oil and score it with a knife to make three or four marks on top.
- Bake in the oven for 30 minutes. It should be nicely crisped and crusty on the outside and still moist inside.
- Serve hot or cold with olive oil and balsamic vinegar for dipping.

Ingredients:

550g strong white flour

120g semi-sun-dried cherry tomatoes marinated in olive oil, herbs and garlic

2 tsp dried thyme

2 tsp dried rosemary

1 tsp salt

1 tbsp tomato puree

7g sachet of fast-action bread yeast

450ml tepid water (boil it first and then let it cool in a jug until it stops furiously steaming)

Olive oil for brushing over and for greasing tin

TEABRACK (HALLOWEEN TEABRACK)

This brack is great for a coffee morning and as an alternative to shop-bought Halloween brack. Traditionally you would place a coin, a matchstick, a ring, a pea and a rag into individual little parcels wrapped in greaseproof paper and get the kids to make a wish as they stir each item in. You need to soak the fruit in the tea overnight.

Method:

- Juice and zest the orange and make up the hot tea. Place the dried fruit in a bowl and pour over the orange juice, orange zest and tea and leave to soak overnight, covered with a tea towel.
- Preheat the oven to 160°C/Gas Mark 4.
- Lightly grease a 2lb loaf tin with a little butter and line the base with parchment paper.
- Beat the butter and brown sugar together, then beat in the egg and the flour.
- Stir in the soaked fruit mixture and pour into the loaf tin.
- Bake for 1 hour. Test the mixture with a skewer and if it comes away clean the cake is cooked.
- Leave to cool in the tin.

Ingredients:

1 orange

225ml hot, strong tea

300g mixed dried fruit

Butter to grease the tin

50g unsalted butter

125g light brown sugar

1 egg

225g self-raising flour

BROWN SCONES

Baking medium- or smaller-sized scones makes more sense than making really big ones as there is a lot of eating in wholemeal flour so these are very filling. I also find that the huge scones you get in some cafes look great but the bread soda is overdone and leaves an aftertaste. This is a wet dough and gives a lovely moist scone. They are ideal with some cheese as a change from sandwiches in school lunchboxes.

Method:

- Preheat the oven to 180°C/Gas Mark 6.
- Lightly grease two baking trays with a little butter.
- Mix the wholemeal flour and plain flour with the salt and bread soda in a large bowl.
- Cut the butter into cubes and crumble together with the flour with your fingertips until it resembles breadcrumbs.
- Make a well in the centre, pour in the buttermilk, and mix well with a fork.
- When the dough is combined, flour your hands and pour the dough out onto a floured board. As the dough is very moist there will be no kneading – just use plenty of flour on your hands to push it, shape it into a ball, and then flatten it out either with your hands or a floured rolling pin to a thickness of approximately 2cm.
- Use a medium-sized round pastry cutter to cut out approximately 10–12 scones.
- Place the scones on the greased baking trays and brush the tops and side with some beaten egg and milk mixed together.
- Bake for 15–20 minutes until nicely risen and golden brown.
- Cool on a wire rack.
- Serve lightly buttered with jam or spread with cream cheese.

Ingredients: – makes 10–12

Butter to grease trays

300g wholemeal flour

150g plain flour

½ tsp salt

1 tsp bread soda

125g unsalted butter

300ml buttermilk

Flour for dusting

1 egg and milk to glaze

CHEESE AND BACON BREAKFAST SCONES

I call these breakfast scones because they are made with rashers, cheese and spring onion, so they are a filling start to the day. Equally good as lunchbox fillers.

Ingredients: – makes 15–20 medium-sized scones

Butter to grease trays

450g self-raising flour

½ tsp baking powder

100g unsalted butter

1 tbsp olive oil

6 rashers

75g cheddar cheese

2 spring onions

2 tbsp wholegrain mustard

1 egg

225ml milk

Flour for dusting and kneading

1 egg and milk to glaze

Method:

- Preheat the oven to 180°C/Gas Mark 6.
- Lightly grease two or three baking trays with a little butter.
- Mix the flour and baking powder in a large bowl. Cut the butter into cubes and crumble into the flour with your fingertips until it resembles breadcrumbs.
- Heat the olive oil in a frying pan over a medium heat and lightly fry the rashers.
- Coarsely grate the cheddar cheese and add to the flour. When the rashers are cooked, use kitchen scissors to trim off the fat and then cut them into small pieces into the flour.
- Rinse the spring onions and cut them into small pieces into the flour.
- Add the mustard and use a fork to mix it with the flour, cheese, rashers and onion.
- Lightly beat the egg and then add it with enough milk to moisten to a soft doughy texture (not too wet – if it is too wet just add a little more flour).
- Gather the dough into a ball with your hands and lightly knead on a floured board.
- Use a lightly floured rolling pin to flatten the dough out to a thickness of approximately 2cm. Use a round pastry cutter to cut out approximately 15–20 scones depending on size.
- Place the scones on the greased baking trays and brush the tops and sides with some beaten egg and milk mixed together.
- Bake for 15–20 minutes until nicely risen and golden brown. Cool on a wire rack.
- Serve them hot or cold, lightly buttered and perhaps with a little more cheese. They also make a great brunch served with some soup.

BLUEBERRY MUFFINS

On one of my summers off from college I worked in a guesthouse on Nantucket Island with my friend Helen, and every morning we would prepare a simple breakfast of warm blueberry muffins and fresh coffee for the guests. They remind me of carefree times, new friendships, blue skies and amazing beaches. Blueberries can be very tart and need a good bit of sugar to sweeten them up. These are great lunchbox fillers.

Method:

- Preheat the oven to 160°C/Gas Mark 4 and line a 12-hole muffin tray with paper muffin cases.
- Melt the butter in a saucepan or in a bowl in the microwave and leave it to cool slightly.
- Sift the flour and baking powder into another bowl and add the caster sugar.
- Rinse the blueberries.
- Beat the eggs in a separate bowl.
- Add the milk to the cooling butter and then add the beaten eggs and the vanilla extract.
- Pour this mixture into the flour and sugar and mix well.
- Fold in the blueberries.
- Spoon the mixture into the cases (or use a jug to pour the mixture) and bake for 20 minutes until risen and golden.
- Cool on a wire rack.

Ingredients: – makes 10–12 muffins

100g unsalted butter

250g self-raising flour

1 tsp baking powder

175g caster sugar

200g blueberries

2 eggs

200ml milk

1 tsp vanilla extract

LEMON AND RASPBERRY MUFFINS

This is my favourite muffin recipe as I love the flavour combination. They are beautiful to look at too, all dressed up in raspberry pink and zesty lemon, and deliciously sweet with a nice balanced hit of lemon.

Method:

- Preheat the oven to 160°C/Gas Mark 4 and line a 12-hole muffin tray with muffin cases.
- Zest and juice the lemon and set aside.
- Rinse the raspberries, dry on a kitchen towel, and set aside.
- Sift the flour and baking powder into a bowl and add the caster sugar.
- Whisk the eggs, sunflower oil and vanilla extract together in a jug, pour this into the dry ingredients and mix.
- Stir in the yoghurt, lemon zest and half of the lemon juice (reserve the other half for glazing) and fold in the raspberries.
- Spoon the mixture into the cases and bake for 15–20 minutes until risen and golden.
- Brush over the tops of the muffins with a glaze made from the icing sugar and the remaining lemon juice and cool on a wire rack.

Ingredients: – makes 10–12 muffins

1 lemon

150g raspberries

250g self-raising flour

2 tsp baking powder

150g caster sugar

2 large eggs

85ml sunflower oil

1 tsp vanilla extract

300g low-fat natural yoghurt

1 tbsp icing sugar

LOW-FAT OAT AND APPLE MUFFINS

These muffins are made moist with grated apples and lifted with cinnamon. Fortified with energising oats, they are perfect for a mid-morning coffee and great lunchbox fillers.

Method:

- Preheat the oven to 160°C/Gas Mark 4 and line a 12-hole muffin tray with muffin cases.
- Sift the flour and baking powder into a bowl and add the muscovado sugar, oats and cinnamon.
- Peel, core and grate the cooking apples, and set aside.
- Whisk the eggs, sunflower oil, yoghurt and vanilla extract together in a large jug, pour into the dry ingredients and stir well.
- Fold in the grated apples.
- Spoon the mixture into the cases and bake for 25–30 minutes until golden.
- Cool on a wire rack.

Ingredients: – makes 10–12 muffins

200g self-raising flour

1 tsp baking powder

150g light muscovado sugar

75g oats

1 tsp cinnamon

2 cooking apples

2 eggs

100ml sunflower oil

300ml low fat natural yoghurt

1 tsp vanilla extract

HONEY BUNS

A plain cupcake needs icing or jam and cream to sweeten it up, but the honey bun is sweet enough on its own. The honey seems to react with the baking powder giving an almost honeycomb texture to these buns which melt in the mouth and are perfect for the sweet-toothed.

Method:

- Preheat the oven to 160°C/Gas Mark 4 and line a cupcake tray with paper cases.
- Using an electric mixer, cream the butter on the lowest setting.
- Gradually add the caster sugar and continue mixing for a few minutes until fluffy.
- Sift the flour into a bowl with the baking powder and cinnamon.
- Add 1 egg to the butter and sugar mixture followed by some of the flour mixture. Continue to mix, alternating between the eggs and flour until all is added.
- Finally add the honey and mix well.
- Spoon the mixture into the cases and bake for 15–20 minutes.
- Leave the buns to cool completely in the cupcake tray and you will probably need to turn it over and bang the base to get them out. During cooking a reaction occurs between the honey, sugar and baking powder to create a lovely crunchy, honeycomb texture. As they rise they tend to spread out and can stick to the edges of the baking tray, and as it can be a little bit of a struggle to get them out of the tin – but worth it – I put them in paper cases as well.

Ingredients: – makes 12–15 honey buns

200g unsalted butter

200g caster sugar

200g self-raising flour

2 tsp baking powder

2 pinches of cinnamon

4 eggs

2 tbsp runny honey

NY CUPCAKES

This is based on the 'Vanilla Vanilla' cupcake from the 'Magnolia Bakery' in New York city; my friend Joanne introduced me to this recipe. Believe me it has been well tested!

Method:

- Preheat the oven to 160°C/Gas Mark 4 and line a cupcake tray with paper cases.
- Using an electric mixer, cream the butter on the lowest setting.
- Gradually add the caster sugar and continue mixing until fluffy.
- Sift the two types of flour into a bowl.
- Add an egg to the butter and sugar mixture followed by a third of the flour, then an egg, a third of the flour, the milk and the last of the flour.
- Finally add the vanilla extract and mix well.
- Spoon the mixture into the cases and bake for 20–25 minutes until golden in colour.
- Cool on a wire rack.
- When cool, ice with the NY vanilla butter-cream icing (see p. 150).

Ingredients: – makes 12–15 large muffin-size cupcakes

100g unsalted butter

225g caster sugar

150g self-raising flour

150g plain flour

2 eggs

125ml milk

1 tsp vanilla extract

DOUBLE CHOCOLATE CUPCAKES

These are always a favourite with kids. They are great for birthday parties when iced, but you can also use them plain for filling lunchboxes.

Method:

- Preheat the oven to 160°C/Gas Mark 4 and line two cupcake trays with paper cases.
- Use an electric mixer to cream the butter on the lowest setting.
- Gradually add the caster sugar and continue mixing until fluffy.
- Sift the flour into a bowl with the baking powder and cocoa powder.
- Add 1 egg to the butter and sugar mixture followed by some of the flour mix. Continue to mix, alternating between the eggs and flour until all is added and then add the vanilla extract.
- Chop the chocolate into small pieces and fold it in with a spatula.
- Spoon the mixture into the cases and bake for 25 minutes.
- Cool on a wire rack.
- When cool ice with chocolate icing (see p. 150) and serve with some rolled chocolate or crumbled chocolate 'Cadbury's Flake'.

Ingredients: – makes 16 generous or 20 medium cupcakes

200g unsalted butter

200g caster sugar

200g self-raising flour

1 tsp baking powder

2 heaped tbsp cocoa powder

4 eggs

1 tsp vanilla extract

50g good chocolate (50% + cocoa content)

CHOCOLATE ICING

Use this icing to give a nice glossy topping to a batch of chocolate cupcakes or to sandwich together the layers of a chocolate cake.

Ingredients: – to cover a batch of cupcakes or a full cake

400g icing sugar

1 heaped tbsp cocoa powder

5 tbsp boiling water

Method:

- Sift the icing sugar and cocoa powder together in a bowl.
- Using a wooden spoon gradually add the water and beat well until smooth.
- Add more water if necessary.
- The icing should have a spreadable consistency but not be runny or watery.

RICH CHOCOLATE BUTTER ICING

For a less sugary and richer, more choco-latey icing.

Ingredients:

100g dark chocolate (70% cocoa content)

250g icing sugar

25g unsalted butter (approx. 1 heaped tbsp)

3 tbsp hot water

Method:

- Break up the chocolate into a bowl and microwave it on low power for 1 to 2 minutes until melted.
- Sift the icing sugar into a bowl and stir in the melted chocolate.
- Add the butter and hot water and beat well with a wooden spoon until smooth.

NY VANILLA BUTTERCREAM ICING

This rich buttercream icing is usually piped on in generous swirls using a piping bag, and calls for a vast amount of icing if you are going to smother each bun. I have also given humbler quantities for regular consumption when just a little of what you fancy will do you good. For pretty pink icing, add a tiny drop of red food colouring.

Ingredients:

150g (or 50g) unsalted butter

650g (or 350g) icing sugar

100ml (or 50ml) milk

2 (or 1) tsp vanilla extract

Method:

- Cream the butter.
- Add two-thirds of the sugar, all the milk and vanilla extract and beat until creamy. Gradually add more of the sugar until the required consistency is achieved (you may not need to use all of the icing sugar).

LUNCHBOX COOKIES

The mixture for these cookies is made in a saucepan and is extremely easy. With energy-giving oats and raisins, these are perfect as lunchbox fillers.

Ingredients: – makes 12 cookies

Butter to grease trays

100g unsalted butter

50g light muscovado sugar

2 tbsp runny honey

½ tsp ground mixed spice

100g self-raising flour

100g oats

50g raisins

Method:

- Preheat the oven to 150°C/Gas Mark 3. Lightly grease and line two baking trays with a little butter and parchment paper.
- Melt the butter, sugar and honey together in a saucepan over a low heat.
- Take off the heat and stir in the mixed spice, sift in the flour, add the oats and raisins, and mix.
- Drop large dollops of the mixture onto the trays, leaving space in between to allow the cookies to spread.
- Bake for 15 minutes. The cookies will be soft when straight out of the oven but will firm up as they cool.
- Leave to cool on a wire tray.

CHOCOLATE CHIP (OR CHUNK) COOKIES

When making chocolate chip cookies my preference is to buy two good bars of chocolate and break them into nice chunky pieces to give the cookies a real chocolatey bite, as chocolate chips can be a little bit miserly. These cookies will keep fresh in an airtight container for a few days, if they last that long. You will need four baking trays as the mixture really spreads out.

Method:

- Preheat the oven to 160°C/Gas Mark 4.
- Lightly grease and line the four baking trays with a little butter and parchment paper.
- Beat the butter, caster sugar and brown sugar together with an electric mixer until light and fluffy.
- Add in the eggs, one at a time.
- Add the vanilla extract.
- Sift in the flour and baking powder and most of the chocolate chips (or chunks), reserving a small handful, and mix well.
- Spoon six round spoonfuls of the mixture onto each baking tray spaced well apart and press the remaining chocolate chips (or chunks) into the top of the cookies.
- Bake for 10–15 minutes until the top is looking settled but the centre is still soft without being too gooey.
- They will harden up as they cool.
- Leave the cookies to cool on the trays and then transfer to a wire rack to cool completely.

Ingredients: – makes 24 to 30 cookies depending on size

Butter to grease trays

225g unsalted butter

200g caster sugar

200g light brown sugar

2 eggs

½ tsp vanilla extract

340g plain flour

2 tsp baking powder

200g good chocolate (50% + cocoa content) cut into chunks or pre-made chocolate chips

SINFULLY HEALTHY CHOCOLATEY NUTTY COOKIES

As a reward for my youngest sister Eimear encouraging her friends to 'like' my gimmetherecipe Facebook page, I promised that I would explore a healthy yet yummy cookie that involved chocolate and nuts. These turned out with more of the texture of a flapjack than a cookie and are definitely aimed at all the nut lovers out there. These are great with a cup of coffee or a glass of milk.

Method:

- Preheat the oven to 160°C/Gas Mark 4 and line three baking trays with parchment paper.
- Chop the chocolate into chunks.
- Place the nuts in a small plastic bag and bash with a rolling pin.
- Use an electric mixer to soften the butter and then mix in the sugar.
- Add the egg and almond (or vanilla) extract to the creamed butter and sugar, mix well and set aside.
- Mix the wholemeal flour, bread soda and baking powder together in a bowl and use a wooden spoon to mix these into the creamed butter mixture, then fold in the crushed nuts, porridge oats and chopped chocolate, and mix well.
- Spoon large dollops of cookie dough spaced well apart onto the trays and shape them with your hand into a roughly circular shape.
- Bake for 10 minutes.
- Leave the cookies to cool on the baking trays for 5 minutes. They will be soft at first but will harden when cool. Transfer to a wire rack to cool completely.

Ingredients: – makes 12 to 20 cookies depending on size

100g dark chocolate

75g mixed nuts (hazelnuts, almonds, pecans, walnuts, brazil nuts)

125g unsalted butter

200g soft brown sugar

1 egg

1 tsp almond extract (or 1 tsp vanilla extract)

100g wholemeal flour

¼ tsp bread soda

¼ tsp baking powder

175g porridge oats

BISCUITS (PLAIN OR CHOCOLATE)

Let the kids have fun using different-shaped cookie cutters to make these biscuits. They are great to make at Christmas time using star and snowman-shaped cutters.

Method:

- Preheat the oven to 170°C/Gas Mark 5 and lightly grease two baking trays with a little butter.
- Use a wooden spoon or electric mixer to cream the butter with the sugar.
- Lightly whisk the egg in a bowl and add a third of it to the creamed butter mixture.
- Sift the flour (and cocoa if using) into a separate bowl and add around a third of it to the creamed butter and sugar followed by more of the egg and flour until it is all added, mixing well between additions.
- Add the vanilla extract and mix well.
- Use your hand to combine the mixture into a heavy dough.
- Lightly flour the worktop and your rolling pin with a dusting of flour to prevent the dough sticking.
- Lightly knead and then roll out the mixture to about the thickness of a euro coin. Use cutters to make shapes and lift them onto a baking tray. Leave room on the tray for spreading.
- Bake the biscuits for 10–12 minutes.
- Leave the biscuits to cool on the tray for a couple of minutes to begin to harden, then lift them onto a wire rack to cool completely.
- Ice and decorate when cool.

Ingredients: – makes 20 biscuits

Butter to grease trays

200g unsalted butter

150g caster sugar

1 egg

250g plain flour

(1 heaped tbsp cocoa powder for chocolate – optional)

½ tsp vanilla extract

Extra flour for dusting, kneading and rolling

TIP: You can buy little packs of coloured food icing pens that are easy for children to hold and squeeze to make eyes and buttons on snowmen cookies, etc.

157

FLORENTINES

I think these are now my favourite biscuits in the world. They are a great way to use up dried raisins, fruit, nuts and seeds and make a beautiful handmade Christmas gift.

Method:

- Preheat the oven to 170°C/Gas Mark 5 and line two baking trays with parchment paper.
- Roughly chop and mix all the dried fruit and nuts together.
- Melt the butter in a saucepan over a low heat, add the caster sugar and golden syrup, and stir well. Add in the porridge oats and flour and stir well.
- Take the saucepan off the heat and stir in all the dried fruit and nuts.
- Use a pastry cutter to shape a spoonful of filling on the baking tray and press down to firm it up. Leave room between the biscuits as they will melt and spread a bit as they cook.
- Bake for 10 minutes and remove from the oven when they are looking golden and starting to crisp at the edges. Allow to cool on the tray for 2 minutes. (They will be soft at first but harden as they cool.)
- Transfer to a baking tray and allow to cool completely.
- Melt the chocolate in a bowl in the microwave (1½ to 2 minutes).
- Add a tiny drop of almond essence (optional) to the melted chocolate and stir well.
- Turn the cooled Florentines upside down and use a teaspoon to coat the underside with melted chocolate. Leave to cool for a few minutes and then use a fork to make swirly lines in the chocolate before leaving to set completely.

Ingredients: – makes 10 large or 20 small biscuits

200g total of mixed dried fruit, nuts (include a good portion of flaked and blanched almonds), seeds and berries. (I used a 70g pack of mixed dried fruit, cranberries, nuts and seeds – available in SuperValu – plus 40g blanched almonds, 40g flaked almonds, 50g combination of dried apricots, glace cherries and candied peel)

50g unsalted butter

50g caster sugar

1 heaped tbsp golden syrup

1 heaped tbsp porridge oats

50g plain flour

150g chocolate (70% cocoa content)

Drop almond essence (optional)

SHORTCRUST PASTRY

Easy to make and very versatile, this pastry base can be used for either sweet or savoury pies, quiches, etc. If your fridge has mysteriously gobbled all of your eggs, you can just use water to bind the pastry, but an egg yolk will make it richer. This quantity of pastry is enough for the top and bottom of a large pie or to make two small quiches in 20cm/8 inch tins.

Ingredients:

250g plain flour

125g butter (cold)

½ tsp salt (savoury pastry) or 25g caster sugar (sweet pastry)

1 egg yolk

3 tbsp cold water

Flour for dusting and kneading, etc.

Method:

- Sift the flour into a bowl, chop the butter into cubes and rub it in with your fingertips until the mixture resembles fine breadcrumbs.
- Stir in the salt or caster sugar and then use a fork to begin to bring the dough together with the egg yolk and the cold water.
- Use your hands to gather the pastry dough into a ball and then knead it lightly on a floured board.
- Shape into a ball, wrap in cling film and press out into a disc shape and leave to rest in the fridge for at least 30 minutes before use.

APPLE OR RHUBARB PIE

I do not know anyone who doesn't like a fruit-filled pie, so it is perfect for a fail-safe dessert. Shortcrust pastry needs time to rest in the fridge before you roll it out, as the pastry will stay together better and be easier to work with after a bit of a chilled rest. Cooking apples will be abundant in the autumn and rhubarb is rampant in the late spring.

Method:

- Make up the shortcrust pastry and leave it to chill in the fridge for at least 30 minutes before using.
- Preheat the oven to 180°C/Gas Mark 6.
- Split the pastry into two and use a lightly floured board and rolling pin to roll each piece out to fit a 24 to 26cm pie dish (a large, deep ovenproof dinner plate also works well).
- Line the base of the pie dish with one half of the pastry.
- Peel, core and chop the apples into the pastry base or rinse and chop in the rhubarb.
- Sprinkle the caster sugar and the cinnamon or ginger over the fruit.
- Beat the egg with the water and use a pastry brush to wet the edges of the pastry base.
- Cover the pie with the second piece of pastry and trim off the excess pastry with a knife.
- Press the edges together with a fork to seal.
- Brush the pastry with the egg wash and score a few steam vents in the top of the pastry with a knife.
- Bake in the oven for 35–40 minutes until golden brown.

Ingredients: – serves 8

1 quantity shortcrust pastry (sweet) (see p. 160)

Flour for dusting and kneading

4 cooking apples or 4 large stalks of rhubarb

50g caster sugar

¼ tsp cinnamon for apple pie or ¼ tsp ginger for rhubarb (if you like it)

1 egg

1 tbsp water

CHOCOLATE AND FRUIT TARTLETS

When you really feel like indulging in a decadent dessert, these are easy to make yet look sophisticated. They are, however, a bit time-consuming as the pastry has to be shaped into individual tartlet tins and chilled before baking blind* and the filling will need time to chill and firm up. Shortcrust pastry needs time to rest in the fridge before you roll it out.

Ingredients: – makes 8–10 depending on size of tartlet trays

1 quantity of shortcrust pastry (sweet) (see p. 160) made adding 1 tbsp cocoa powder

Flour for dusting and kneading

150g good quality chocolate (50%+ cocoa content)

150ml double cream

50ml milk

200g fresh fruit – strawberries, raspberries, blueberries

Method:

Pastry cases

- Make up the shortcrust pastry with the addition of 1 tablespoon of cocoa powder when adding the flour and leave it to chill in the fridge wrapped in cling film for at least 30 minutes before using.
- Preheat the oven to 180°C/Gas Mark 6.
- Lightly knead the pastry on a floured board and cut it in half (it's easier to work with that way).
- Roll out one half to the size of a large plate. Lay the rolled pastry on top of a tartlet tin and press it down into it to line it, then trim it at the edges. Continue like this to line the tartlet trays. (This should line four or five depending on their size.)
- Do the same with the other half of the pastry if you have enough tartlet trays, if not do them in batches.
- Place the pastry-lined tartlet tins in the fridge to chill for 15 minutes. (This will reduce shrinkage.)
- Prick the base of the pastry all over with a fork then cover with parchment paper and fill with pie weights or baking beans to weigh it down.
- Bake the pastry bases in the preheated oven for 10 minutes. Remove the beans and parchment paper and return the pastry case to the oven for 5 minutes until very lightly coloured.
- Leave the tartlets to cool in the tins and then remove.

Chocolate filling:

- Break the chocolate up into a bowl.
- Boil the cream and milk together, then pour onto the broken chocolate stirring well for a smooth mixture. Place in the fridge until cooling, but still fluid enough to pour into the tartlet cases.
- Fill each tartlet with the chocolate and chill in the fridge for at least 1 hour before serving.
- To serve crumble a 'Cadbury's Flake' over the tartlets and decorate with scattered raspberries or blueberries or sliced strawberries.

TIP: Any leftover chocolate mixture can be made into truffles. Add a splash of brandy and allow it to harden in the fridge, then use a melon baller or teaspoon and your hands to shape it into small balls and roll them in crumbled 'Cadbury's Flake'.

*Blind baking: This is when you partially bake the pastry before filling it so that it gets a chance to begin to cook and doesn't go soggy.

WICKED CHOCOLATE BROWNIES

Brownies appear to have their origins in America, but are a worldwide baking favourite. Be careful not to overcook the brownies as you want the centre meltingly soft and moist. As I am a big fan of chocolate I like to chop some extra chunks to push into the mix when it has been poured into the tray.

Method:

- Preheat the oven to 160°C/Gas Mark 4 and lightly grease and line a 33 x 25cm baking tray with a little butter and parchment paper.
- Break up 300g of the chocolate (reserve 50g for later), cube the butter and melt them together in a bowl in the microwave (low power 1 to 2 minutes) or over a saucepan of warm water.
- Gradually add the sugar and stir well.
- Sift in the flour and stir well.
- Lightly whisk the eggs in a bowl and then stir into the cooling chocolate mixture until smooth.
- Pour the brownie mixture into the baking tray, break up the reserved 50g of chocolate, and press it in here and there.
- Bake for 25 minutes until the top is looking settled but the centre is still soft without being too gooey. Test with a wooden toothpick or skewer – some mixture will cling to it but if it runs off give it a little extra cooking time – you want a moist texture.
- Leave to cool, dust with icing sugar and cut into brownie squares.

Ingredients: – makes 16 to 20

Butter to grease tin

350g dark chocolate (55% + cocoa content)

275g unsalted butter

300g caster sugar

200g plain flour

4 eggs

Icing sugar to dust

TIP: If you use a very high cocoa content, e.g. 85%, then you will get a lot more portions, as a little piece will have more than enough of a hit for even the most raving chocoholic.

VICTORIA SPONGE CAKE

This is an old-fashioned classic teatime cake, perfect sandwiched together with raspberry jam and whipped cream.

Method:

- Preheat the oven to 170°C/Gas Mark 5.
- Grease and line the base of two round 20cm cake tins with a little butter and a round of parchment paper.
- Use an electric mixer to cream the butter and the sugar together.
- Sift the flour and the baking powder together in a separate bowl.
- Gradually add the flour and the eggs to the butter mix, alternating between both until all are added.
- Finally mix in the milk and divide the mixture between the two tins.
- Bake the cakes for 20 minutes.
- Test by gently pressing the cake – if it bounces back it is done.
- Remove from the tins and cool on a wire tray.
- Whip the cream, cover one side of the cake with jam and cream and place the other half on top.
- Lightly sprinkle with icing sugar.

Ingredients: – serves 8

Butter to grease tin

200g unsalted butter

200g caster sugar

200g self-raising flour

1 tsp baking powder

4 eggs

2 tbsp milk

For filling:

Small carton of fresh cream

Raspberry jam

Icing sugar to dust on top

TIP: Use loose-bottomed or springform cake tins for ease of removal.

CHOCOLATE AND RASPBERRY BIRTHDAY CAKE

I like to add some chopped raspberries to the cake mix and to sandwich it together with a layer of chocolate icing and raspberries in the middle, but you can leave them out if you wish. I then encase it in more chocolate icing and decorate it with chocolate buttons, raspberries and sliced strawberries. Use springform or loose-bottomed cake tins if you can, as they make it much easier when it comes to getting the cake out of the tins.

Ingredients:

Butter to grease tin

2 tbsp cocoa powder, heaped

5 tbsp warm water

200g unsalted butter

200g caster sugar

200g self-raising flour

2 tsp baking powder

4 eggs

12 raspberries for cake mix

Chocolate icing to decorate (see p. 150)

Raspberries to decorate

Strawberries to decorate

Chocolate buttons to decorate

Method:

- Preheat the oven to 170°C/Gas Mark 5.
- Grease and line two round cake tins (20cm or 8 inches) with a little butter and parchment paper.
- Mix up the cocoa with the warm water in a cup and set aside to cool a little until needed.
- Use an electric mixer to cream the butter and sugar together.
- Sift the flour and baking powder together in a separate bowl and set aside.
- Beat the eggs in a bowl and add about a third of the beaten eggs to the butter and sugar mix, followed by about a third of the flour. Continue adding the next third of the egg and then the flour, alternating until all are added.
- Mix in 12 roughly chopped raspberries, then add the cooled cocoa and mix well.
- Divide the mixture between the two cake tins. Bake the cakes for 30–35 minutes, testing with a skewer to see if it is baked – if any wet mixture clings to the skewer return to the oven for a further 5 minutes and test again.

- Remove the cakes from the tins and cool on a wire rack tray before icing.
- Fill the centre with chocolate icing and sliced berries and smooth more chocolate icing all over the top and sides before decorating with more berries and chocolate buttons.

TIP: If you do not have time to make icing just sandwich the cake together with some jam and dust over the top with icing sugar.

BERRY COULIS

I particularly like the combination of raspberries and chocolate, and this coulis could be used to add an extra decorative swirl to a slice of chocolate cake or chocolate and fruit tartlets. Strictly speaking, a coulis should be strained with a sieve so that it is smooth. I prefer to retain the goodness of the seeds and pulp of the fruit by using a blender to puree it instead. (Well OK, I just could not be bothered to strain it and it tastes fine to me.)

Ingredients:
125g raspberries or any berries such as blackberries, strawberries, blueberries
25g caster sugar
A little water

Method:
- Heat the berries in a saucepan with the caster sugar and a little water and stir well so that the sugar dissolves and the berries soften.
- Use a blender to puree into a lovely sweet syrupy coulis.

CHOCOLATE CHIP SQUARES

What I love about making this cake is that there is no need to haul out the electric mixer to cream the butter, as you melt it in a saucepan and add in all of the ingredients to make a wonderful syrupy batter that flows to all four corners of a baking tray when you pour it in. This is a cake that is perfect for entertaining a crowd and I serve it straight from the baking tray.

Method:

- Preheat the oven to 160°C/Gas Mark 4.
- Grease a 32 x 20cm baking tray with a little butter and line the base with parchment paper.
- Melt the butter in a large saucepan over a low heat and then take it off the heat and leave to cool for 5 minutes.
- Lightly beat the eggs in a bowl.
- Add the brown sugar, golden syrup, beaten eggs and vanilla extract to the melted butter and beat with a wooden spoon until the mixture is smooth.
- Sift in the flour and cocoa powder and then stir in 100g of the chocolate chips (1 pack).
- Spread the mixture on the tray and bake for 25–30 minutes.
- Test the mixture with a skewer and if it comes away clean the cake is cooked.
- When cool decorate the cake with a thick layer of chocolate icing generously scattered with the remaining chocolate chips.
- Cut into squares to serve.

Ingredients: – makes 15

Butter to grease tray

250g unsalted butter

3 eggs

250g light golden brown sugar

50ml or 3 tbsp golden syrup

1 tsp vanilla extract

200g self-raising flour

50g or 7 tbsp cocoa powder

2 x 100g packs of chocolate chips (1 for decorating)

Chocolate icing to decorate (see p. 150)

BLACK FOREST ROULADE

This is a luxurious alternative to the traditional Christmas Chocolate Log and is great as a birthday cake too. Macerate the cherries overnight in the Crème de Cassis for extra flavour. I use Crème de Cassis because that is what is available in my local supermarket and it works just as well as Kirsch, which is traditionally used to make Black Forest Gateau.

Ingredients: for cake

Butter to grease tray

200g dark chocolate (70% cocoa) (25g is for
    decorating)

6 large eggs

75g caster sugar

75g light muscovado sugar

Icing sugar to dust

Grated chocolate for decoration

For filling and syrup:

1 x 425g can of pitted black cherries in heavy syrup

100ml Crème de Cassis or Kirsch

125g caster sugar (for syrup)

300ml tub whipping cream

Method:

- Soak the cherries in their syrup and the Crème de Cassis or Kirsch overnight.
- Preheat the oven to 160°C/Gas Mark 4 and grease and line a baking tray with a little butter and parchment paper.
- Break up and melt 175g of the chocolate in a bowl in the microwave (1½ to 2 minutes) and set aside.
- Separate the egg yolks from the egg whites.
- Beat the egg yolks, caster sugar and muscovado sugar together until thick and pale.
- Separately use an electric whisk to beat the egg whites until thick enough to stand in peaks.
- Stir the melted chocolate into the egg yolk and sugar mixture.
- Use a metal spoon to fold the egg whites into the egg yolk and chocolate mixture. Stir gently to combine, do not over beat.
- Pour onto a 33 x 25cm baking tray and bake for 15 minutes.
- When cooked cover with a clean sheet of parchment paper and a damp tea towel and leave to cool for 2 minutes.

- Take off the tea towel but leave the parchment and use a knife to loosen the edges of the cake.
- Turn the tray upside down onto a board, remove the tray and peel away the parchment paper on the base of the cake.
- Replace with a clean sheet of parchment paper and starting at one end roll up the cake with the parchment paper inside.
- Leave to cool completely, covered with the damp tea towel.
- Make the syrup by straining off all the syrup and liquor from the cherries into a saucepan with 125g of caster sugar.
- Bring to the boil until bubbling and thick, for a few minutes.
- Remove from the heat and cool.
- Whip the cream.
- Fill the log by unrolling it and removing the parchment paper, then drizzle over the syrup, scatter the cherries and smooth over the cream.
- Gently roll up again and dust with icing sugar and grated chocolate.

PEACH AND RASPBERRY BATTER CAKE

This golden cake is baked on a baking tray and is great for entertaining a crowd. I generally use canned peaches, but if you can get hold of some juicy fresh ripe ones to slice up all the better.

Method:

- Preheat the oven to 160°C/Gas Mark 4 and grease and line a 33 x 25cm baking tray with a little butter and parchment paper.
- Melt the butter in a large saucepan and take off the heat to cool for 5 minutes.
- Meanwhile, rinse the raspberries and strain off the juice from the peaches (reserve the juice for serving).
- Beat the eggs in a bowl and set aside.
- Put the brown sugar and golden syrup into the saucepan with the cooling melted butter and mix well. Mix in the beaten eggs, vanilla extract and sift in the flour and mix well until smooth.
- Spread the mixture in the baking tray and lay the peach slices evenly over the top. Scatter the raspberries over the top and then bake for 40 minutes turning the oven down to 140°C/Gas Mark 3 for the last 15 minutes.
- The fruit will gradually sink and the batter will rise as it cooks, with the fruit ending up mostly covered but with nice colourful pieces poking through.
- Test the mixture with a skewer and if it comes away clean the cake is cooked.
- Cool and serve from the tray with whipped cream and the peach juice.

Ingredients:

Butter to grease tray

250g unsalted butter

125g fresh raspberries

2 x 400g cans of sliced peaches in juice

3 eggs

250g light golden brown sugar

50ml golden syrup

1 tsp vanilla extract

250g self-raising flour

TIP: For a big crowd bake two of these the day before and cover with tinfoil until needed. Layer one on top of the other sandwiched together with more raspberries and cream in the middle and dust over with icing sugar.

I played around with a lot of cheesecake recipes until I devised one with a filling that I really like. It is lent a bit of lightness with the jelly and indulgence is still ensured with the addition of whipped cream. My eldest child Johnnie came up with the idea of using Oreo cookies in the base and this goes down really well with kids. Ideally make this the night before as it needs a couple of hours to set properly.

DOUBLE STRAWBERRY AND OREO CHEESECAKE
LEMON, RASPBERRY AND OREO CHEESECAKE

Ingredients:

28 Oreo cookies (2 x 154g pack)

75g unsalted butter

135g packet lemon or strawberry jelly

100ml cold water

150ml cream

450g Philadelphia cream cheese (2 x 225g pack)

50g icing sugar

Lemon version

1 lemon and handful of raspberries

Lemon zest to decorate

Fresh raspberries to decorate

Strawberry version

1 x 400g can of strawberries in syrup

Fresh strawberries

25g grated chocolate (70% cocoa content to decorate)

Method:

- Preheat the oven to 160°C/Gas Mark 4.
- Put the Oreo cookies in a plastic bag and crush into crumbs with a rolling pin or blitz in a mini chopper.
- Melt the butter, combine with the cookie crumbs, and mix well.
- Press the cookie mix into the base of the 23cm springform cake tin and compact well together with the back of a spoon.
- Bake in the oven for 10 minutes, take out and leave to cool. Switch off the oven.
- Put the jelly in a microwave-proof jug with 100ml cold water and microwave for 1 minute. Mix well until fully dissolved.
- Bring the level of the jelly up to 400ml in the jug by adding in either the juice of the lemon and cold water or the strawberry syrup from the can of strawberries (depending on which version you are making).
- Place the jelly in the fridge to set for 1 hour.
- Lightly whip the cream until just beginning to form peaks and set aside.
- Use an electric mixer to cream the Philadelphia cheese and semi-set jelly together with the icing sugar until smooth.
- Fold the cream and strained canned strawberries or a handful of fresh raspberries into the cheesecake mix and pour over the Oreo cookie base.
- Leave to set for a few hours or ideally overnight.
- Serve decorated with fresh strawberries and grated chocolate or fresh raspberries and lemon zest.

PEAR TIRAMISU

This is a cross between a 'Poire Belle Hélène' and a tiramisu. I love using fruit in dessert and the chocolate and pears add another dimension to this lightweight version of the Italian classic that is equally tasty and very simple to prepare. This is a no-cook dessert that is child's play to make, but made with coffee it is most definitely for the grown ups. I make this in a large deep square dish 25 x 25cm. If you want to make a child-friendly version use some cooled hot chocolate instead of the coffee.

Method:

- Mix the mascarpone with the yoghurt, caster sugar and vanilla extract and stir well.
- Mix the cinnamon into the cold coffee in a bowl for dipping into.
- Grate the chocolate and set aside.
- Dip half of the sponge fingers into the cold coffee and place them in the base of the serving dish.
- Spread half of the mascarpone mixture on top.
- Open, drain and slice the canned pears (reserve a couple of slices for decorating the top) and arrange them generously on top of the mascarpone and sprinkle over most of the grated chocolate.
- Dip and layer the remaining sponge fingers and spread the rest of the mascarpone mixture over them.
- Arrange the reserved pear on top and sprinkle with the remaining grated chocolate.
- Cover the dish with cling film and leave to chill in the fridge for at least 1 hour before serving.

Ingredients: – serves: 16 +

500g mascarpone (Italian cream cheese)

500g Greek yoghurt

80g caster sugar

2 tsp vanilla extract

½ tsp cinnamon

400ml cold strong coffee

50g chocolate (70% cocoa content)

50 sponge finger biscuits (I used a pack and a half of boudoir sponge fingers – 200g per pack)

2 x 410g cans of pear halves in own juice

APPLE AND BLACKBERRY PUDDING

This is a delicious soft and fruity pudding and a great way to use freshly picked blackberries. It also works well with a combination of ripe peaches and blueberries.

Method:

- Preheat the oven to 180˚C/Gas Mark 6 and grease a baking or pudding dish 25 x 25cm with butter.
- Heat the butter and cream together in a saucepan and bring to the boil. Leave to cool a little.
- Whisk the caster sugar and the eggs together for a few minutes until they have formed a thick, battery mixture and set aside.
- Prepare the fruit by coring, peeling and slicing the apples into rings, and washing the blackberries.
- Add the butter and cream mixture to the eggs and sugar mixture, and whisk together.
- Gently fold in the sifted flour to make a thick batter.
- Pour the mixture into the baking dish and push in the apple rings.
- Scatter the blackberries over the top and push some of them down into the batter.
- Bake for 45–50 minutes and test the mixture with a skewer – if it comes away clean the pudding is cooked.
- Great served hot, straight from the oven, with some cream.

Ingredients: – serves 9

Butter to grease the dish

175g unsalted butter

250ml carton of whipping cream

225g caster sugar

3 eggs

400g cooking apples (2 large or 3 medium)

300g blackberries

300g plain flour

STICKY PEAR AND APPLE CRUMBLE

This crumble recipe is sticky, chewy and sweet and with a combination of oats, wholemeal and plain flour is almost healthy if you can forget about all the sugar!

Method:

- Preheat the oven to 170°C/Gas Mark 5.
- Peel and chop the fruit into smallish pieces and cook in a saucepan with a splash of water and the caster sugar over a medium heat until softening (still with a bit of bite and not a pulp). This takes about 5 minutes.
- Put the plain and wholemeal flours and the oats into a mixing bowl and chop in the butter.
- Use your fingertips to crumble the flour, oats and butter together until it starts to resemble breadcrumbs.
- Add the brown sugar and mix well with a fork.
- Place the cooked fruit in a large greased baking dish and scatter the crumble mixture on top – press it down lightly but do not over-compact it.
- Bake for 35–40 minutes.
- Delicious on its own, even better with custard or vanilla ice-cream.

Ingredients:

2kgs fruit – roughly 4 to 5 medium-sized cooking apples and 4 to 5 small ripe pears

50g caster sugar (for cooking the fruit)

100g plain flour

50g wholemeal flour

50g porridge oats

100g unsalted butter

200g light golden brown sugar

Butter to grease dish

APPLE AND BLUEBERRY LOAF CAKE

This loaf cake is high on fruit content and amazingly moist and as my mother-in-law Kitty says, 'There's great cutting in it.' The blueberries' juice oozes out of the fruit as they cook, giving a beautiful damson-coloured marbling throughout the cake. There will appear to be very little batter to cover the fruit, but bake it and be amazed.

Method:
- Preheat the oven to 180°C/Gas Mark 6.
- Lightly grease a 26cm 2lb loaf tin with a little butter and line the base with parchment paper.
- Cream the butter with the caster sugar using an electric mixer.
- Beat in the eggs and then sift in the flour and mix well.
- Prepare the apples by peeling, coring and chopping them into small pieces.
- Mix the apples and blueberries into the mixture and pour into the tin.
- Bake for 40–45 minutes and test the cake with a skewer. If it comes away clean the cake is cooked.
- Leave to cool for 10 minutes before removing from the tin.
- This cake does not need any accompaniment except for a cup of tea, and is served in slices.

Ingredients:
Butter to grease tin

75g unsalted butter

125g caster sugar

2 eggs

250g self-raising flour

2 medium-sized cooking apples

125g blueberries

EVE'S PUDDING

I remember making this classic dessert in my Home Economics class in school. Lovely softened and sweetened apples are hidden under a cushion of soft, moist sponge cake.

Method:

- Preheat the oven to 180°C/Gas Mark 6.
- Peel, core and chop the apples into a saucepan with the lemon juice and water.
- Stir well and cook over medium heat with a lid on for a few minutes until the apples are soft. Keep an eye on the apples though, as they will cook very quickly in very little liquid and begin to stick to the pan.
- Add the 3 tablespoons of caster sugar and 30g of the butter to the softened apples. Stir well and transfer to a greased 25 x 25cm baking dish.
- While the apples cool, use an electric mixer to cream the remaining 150g of butter and then add the 200g of caster sugar, continuing to mix until light and fluffy.
- Sift in the flour and add in the eggs (alternating between a third of each until all are added).
- Spoon the cake mixture over the apples and bake in the oven for 30 minutes until golden in colour.
- Great served hot with warm custard or ice-cream.

Ingredients:

3 large cooking apples

Juice of ½ lemon

3 tbsp water

200g plus 3 tbsp caster sugar

180g unsalted butter

Butter to grease dish

200g self-raising flour

3 eggs

CHOCOLATE, COFFEE AND ALMOND (OR VANILLA) MOUSSE

I once made the mistake of buying almond extract instead of vanilla and decided to use it anyway. It really gives this mousse such an unbelievable kick that it is paradoxically intense and light at the same time. Because it is so intense, I recommend making this in small-portion containers such as good-looking egg cups. This is most definitely NOT a child-friendly dessert, so reserve this one for dinner parties.

Method:

- Preheat the oven to 200°C/Gas Mark 7 and put the almonds in to roast for 5–10 minutes – keep a close eye on them so that they do not burn. (The mousse is not cooked so turn the oven off afterwards.)
- Let the roasted almonds cool and then put them into a small plastic bag and bash them to a crumb with a rolling pin and reserve for decorating.
- Mix the coffee granules with the almond (or vanilla) extract and 2 tablespoons of boiling water and set aside.
- Roughly chop the chocolate, place it in a bowl and melt it in the microwave or over a pan of hot water. Stir in the coffee and almond mixture and another 2 tablespoons of water to thin out the chocolate and set aside to cool a little.
- Whisk the egg whites to soft peaks, then whisk the caster sugar into the egg whites until thick and set aside.
- Stir the Greek yoghurt into the cooling chocolate.
- Carefully fold the egg-white mixture into the chocolate mix using a metal spoon, taking care not to over mix. Spoon into small ramekins or egg cups and chill for a couple of hours or overnight.
- Serve the mousse with the crumbled roast almonds sprinkled on top.

Ingredients:

Very small handful of almonds for roasting and decorating

½ tsp coffee granules

½ tsp almond extract (or vanilla if you're not a fan of almonds)

4 tbsp boiling water

100g dark chocolate (70%+ cocoa content)

2 egg whites

1 tbsp caster sugar

50g Greek yoghurt

Fruit and cream make for delicious desserts and adding meringue introduces a wonderful crunchy texture. I use a light golden brown sugar in this recipe which results in turning the meringue a lovely toffee colour.

STRAWBERRY AND HAZELNUT TOFFEE PAVLOVA

Ingredients:

For the meringue

3 large egg whites

175g light golden brown sugar

For the filling:

Handful of hazelnuts

500g strawberries

2 tbsp icing sugar

250ml carton of fresh cream

250g natural fromage frais

Method:

- Preheat the oven to 200°C/Gas Mark 7 and roast the hazelnuts in a hot oven until browned. Wrap the hazelnuts in a tea towel and rub to remove as much of the skin as possible. Place the cooled hazelnuts in a small plastic bag and bash with a rolling pin to crush them.
- Reduce the oven heat to 150°C/Gas Mark 3 for the meringue. Line a baking tray with parchment paper.
- Whisk the egg whites with an electric mixer until beginning to stiffen up. Add in the brown sugar about a tablespoon at a time, continuing to mix until all is added.
- Use a metal spoon to spread a circular base of meringue about the size of a small dinner plate and 1cm in height onto the parchment paper. Then spoon large dollops of the meringue mixture next to each other around the edge of the base to form the meringue shell wall. Use a skewer to make a swirl in each round blob and lift it up slightly. (This gives the blobs nicely tipped peaks.)
- Put the meringue into the oven and turn the heat down low to 130°C/Gas Mark 2 and leave for 1 hour. Turn off the oven and leave the meringue base inside until cold.
- Remove the meringue base from the oven and peel off the parchment paper.
- Fill the meringue before serving. Blitz a small handful of the strawberries in a food processor or mini chopper, with 1 tablespoon of icing sugar to make a puree.
- Whisk the cream with an electric mixer until stiffening and then stir in the fromage frais and the other tablespoon of icing sugar.
- Slice the remaining strawberries. Spoon a layer of the cream mix into the meringue base and top with half of the strawberries. Spoon the remaining cream on top, then decorate with the strawberries, crushed hazelnuts and puree.

DINNER PARTY (AND OTHER SPECIAL OCCASIONS)

- Starters and Nibbles
- Side Dishes
- Dinner Party Mains

DINNER PARTY (AND OTHER SPECIAL OCCASIONS)

The dinner party should not be dreaded, but it invariably is. Not only do you have to clean the house, but you also have to produce some masterpiece in the kitchen while coercing a child out of tree-climbing clothes into something more respectable. These expectations are generally self-imposed and cause undue pressure, but there is no escaping from the fact that dinner parties usually end up being stressful affairs and things can get fairly explosive in the kitchen. I have been there. You're just about to plate up, having somehow managed to get everything cooked at the same time, and then a child breaks a wine glass or sets fire to the napkins with the candles.

Delegation is something that most of us need to work on. A dinner party should be more than a one man/woman show. There are plenty of jobs that can be done by children, significant others or anyone else willing to lend a hand, e.g. hoovering, setting the table, finding candles, etc. I operate on a rewards system (also known as bribery) and have no problem in making payments in bars of chocolate or later bedtimes.

The key to a successful dinner party will be to keep it simple, and this section of the book provides canapés and side dishes that can be made ahead of time and some one-pot dishes for mains. This section also includes a planning schedule and suggested menu for family gatherings such as communions and birthdays, as well as a time planner for Christmas Day.

One big tip that I can give you for a dinner party is to bake or buy some fresh bread. People go to terrible trouble making finicky canapés whereas the clever restaurant people will always bring a basket of bread to your table. Your guests will probably arrive famished and nothing will take the edge off the hunger like a slice of tasty brown bread and butter.

Lastly, remind yourself that you are not inviting people to your home to impress them, but to enjoy their company and have a good time.

RED PEPPER HUMMUS DIP WITH CRUDITÉS

Chickpeas are high in protein and that makes hummus very popular with vegetarians. On their own chickpeas are bland, so hummus needs something to give it a good kick of flavour. Traditional hummus recipes using lemon juice, garlic and tahini (sesame seed) paste are OK, but still on the bland side, so I came up with the idea of blitzing in a roasted red pepper instead and it works. Hummus can be made up to a day in advance if it is covered and stored in the fridge. If you want to do the vegetables in advance then these can be stored in the fridge in a ziplock bag for up to a day.

Method:

- Preheat the oven to 200°C/Gas Mark 7 and roast the red pepper until the skin gets black and charred. This takes about 30 minutes. When the pepper is blackened, place it in a small plastic sandwich bag until cool and then peel off the skin and deseed.
- Peel the carrots, rinse the celery and cucumber, and cut all of them into batons.
- Drain and rinse the chickpeas using a sieve.
- Peel and crush the garlic.
- Use a food processor to blitz together the chickpeas, garlic, Greek yoghurt, olive oil, roasted red pepper and cayenne pepper.
- If it is too thick, add a little more Greek yoghurt.
- Serve in a bowl with the vegetable batons arranged for dipping.

Ingredients:

1 red pepper

3 carrots

3 celery stalks

1 cucumber

1 x 220g can of chickpeas

1 garlic clove

2 tbsp Greek yoghurt

1 tsp olive oil

1 tsp cayenne pepper

TIP: If you are not a fan of red peppers then try my Caramelised Red Onion Hummus instead, which my daughter Ellie rates as 'savage'. Soften two thinly sliced red onions in 1 tablespoon of olive oil for 10 minutes on a low heat. Add 2 tablespoons of dark muscovado sugar and 2 tablespoons of balsamic vinegar and cook for 5 minutes on a medium heat. Blitz with drained and rinsed chickpeas, a garlic clove, 3 tablespoons of Greek yoghurt and 1 teaspoon of olive oil.

CREAMY GUACAMOLE

Guacamole is a deliciously fresh and zingy dip. If you prefer a creamier texture, add a little more Greek yoghurt. This dip does not keep so well and should be made no longer than an hour in advance of use.

Ingredients:

1 medium red onion

1 garlic clove

Juice of 1 lime

2 avocados

2 tbsp Greek yoghurt

Sea salt and ground black pepper for seasoning

Method:

- Peel and finely chop the red onion.
- Peel and crush the garlic. Juice the lime.
- Cut the avocados in half and take out the stones. Use a spoon to scoop out the flesh.
- Mash the avocado flesh together with the red onion, garlic, lime juice and Greek yoghurt.
- Season with salt and black pepper.
- Great served as a dip with pitta chips (see p. 197).

TIP: When buying avocados do not buy if they are hard or overly soft. If you wish to use them straight away there should be a slight give in the flesh when lightly squeezed. If you do buy them hard and want to speed up the ripening process, place them in a brown paper bag at room temperature for two to five days.

SALSA FRESCA

Salsa means sauce and can be anything you want it to be. If you are after a Salsa Verde then you really should keep it green. Salsa Fresca means fresh and it is the bunch of parsley that brings the freshness to this salsa. Cherry tomatoes are usually lovely and sweet and will balance the heat of the chilli. This can be made a day in advance and will keep well for two days stored covered in the fridge.

Ingredients:

1 red chilli

300g cherry tomatoes

Bunch of flat-leaf parsley

4–5 spring onions

Sea salt and ground black pepper for seasoning

Method:

- Deseed and finely chop the red chilli.
- Rinse and quarter the cherry tomatoes.
- Finely chop the parsley and slice the spring onions.
- Combine all the ingredients together, mix well and season with salt and black pepper.
- Serve as a refreshing summer dip with a bowl of pitta chips (see p. 197).

TIP: If you cannot get flat-leaf parsley, a mixture of coriander and curly parsley finely chopped works well too.

CUCUMBER DIP (RAITA)

Cucumber and mint have lovely cooling properties and a spoonful of this is great with a hot curry. It is also good for dipping with pitta chips (below) or with lamb dishes such as koftas (p. 211).

Ingredients:

1 cucumber

400g natural yoghurt

2 tsp fresh mint

Method:

- Peel and dice the cucumber and mix with the yoghurt and chopped fresh mint.
- Refrigerate until ready to use.
- Serve with pitta chips.

PITTA CHIPS

These crisps are great with any of the dips such as guacamole, pesto and hummus or to scoop up a cherry tomato salsa. This quantity will make one trayful of chips.

Ingredients:

4 round pitta breads

Olive oil for drizzling

2 tsp paprika

Sea salt and ground pepper to season

Method:

- Preheat the oven to 200°C/Gas Mark 7.
- Use kitchen scissors to cut the pitta breads into triangular wedges and then snip the edges so they are single layered.
- Place the cut pitta on a baking tray and drizzle with olive oil.
- Season with a generous sprinkling of the paprika and salt and pepper.
- Give the tray a good shake.
- Bake in the oven until crisp for approximately 10 minutes, giving the tray another good shake halfway through cooking.

SMOKED SALMON, LETTUCE AND CREAM CHEESE WRAPS

My kids love these and as well as being easy nibbles to serve at a party, they are also a great way of using up leftover smoked salmon and are very welcome in the lunchbox.

Ingredients: – makes 40 to 50 mini bites

5 large soft flour tortillas

Philadelphia cream cheese for spreading

Iceberg lettuce

400g smoked salmon

2 lemons

Method:

- Generously spread each tortilla with the cream cheese.
- Top with a layer of shredded lettuce and then salmon.
- Tightly roll up the wrap and cut each diagonally into about eight to ten pieces.
- Serve with lemon wedges on the side.

197

CHILLI BEEF NACHOS

This dish is an assembly of the various elements: chilli beef, salsa, tortilla chips and cheese. Why not make the chilli con carne the night before and that will leave you with very little to do.

Method:

- Make the chilli con carne and the salsa fresca. If you have made the chilli con carne earlier, reheat it thoroughly in a saucepan on the hob before assembling the Nachos to ensure it is properly heated through.
- Preheat the oven to 200˚C/Gas Mark 7.
- Grate the cheddar cheese and set aside.
- Divide the salsa fresca evenly into the base of two 25 x 25cm baking dishes and top both with the chilli con carne.
- Chop up the jalapenos and scatter them on top of the chilli, followed by the tortilla chips.
- Top with the grated cheddar cheese.
- Heat in the oven for 5–10 minutes until the cheese has melted.
- Serve with a side of guacamole and a dish of sour cream.

Ingredients: – serves 12+ as a starter portion

1 quantity chilli con carne (see p. 91)

1 quantity salsa fresca (see p. 196)

150g cheddar cheese

15–20 sliced green jalapenos from jar

2 x 175g bags corn tortilla chips

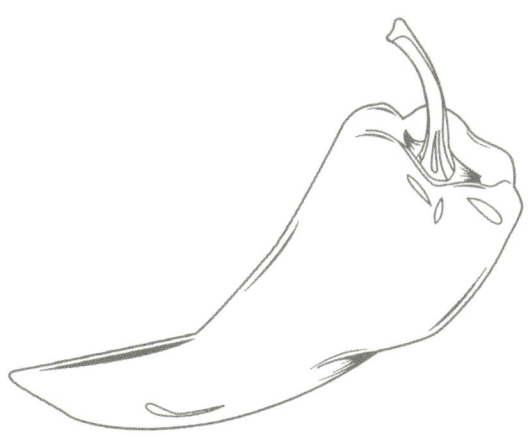

CHERRY TOMATO AND CHILLI JAM

A batch of this will almost fill two jam jars. Chilli jam is great served as a relish with cheese and crackers or with tortilla chips for dipping. Sterilise the jam jar with some boiling water and it should keep in the fridge for at least a week. It does not matter what type of brown sugar you use, but generally the darker it is the deeper the flavour.

Method:

- I like to prepare the ingredients to some degree before blitzing them as I feel that they will integrate better with the other ingredients and be more evenly mixed together.
- Deseed and roughly chop the red chillies.
- Crush the garlic.
- Peel and grate the ginger.
- Cut the cherry tomatoes in half
- Use a food processor or mini chopper to combine the chillies, garlic, ginger and tomatoes together with the raisins. Blitz it well to break down the raisins.
- Put this tomato mixture into a saucepan with the fish sauce, red wine vinegar and brown sugar.
- Mix well, bring to the boil then reduce to a simmer over a low heat for 30 minutes, stirring occasionally.
- Allow the chilli jam to cool and then spoon it into sterilised jam jars, making sure it is cool before refrigerating.

Ingredients:

2 red chillies

2 garlic cloves

3cm thumb-width piece of ginger

300g ripe cherry tomatoes

50g raisins

1 tbsp fish sauce (nam pla)

50ml red wine vinegar

200g dark brown sugar

OLIVE AND FETA OR MOZZARELLA BITES

These are simple yet very attractive-looking bites. Mozzarella pearls are stocked in some supermarkets. Alternatively you could use a melon baller to make your own from a large mozzarella ball; I've tried it though and it's a bit fiddly and time-consuming. If you cannot get hold of mozzarella pearls either substitute with mozzarella chunks or squares of feta if time/patience is an issue. Don't make these too far in advance of use or the basil will wilt.

Method:

- Slice the olives in two and cut the sun-dried tomatoes into slivers big enough to thread onto the cocktail sticks.
- Tear the basil into pieces.
- Assemble the canapés, ensuring that each cocktail stick gets at least one piece of mozzarella, semi-sun-dried tomato, olive and basil.
- Serve drizzled with olive oil and seasoned with a little salt and black pepper.

Ingredients:

150g mixture of green and black stoned olives

120g tub semi-sun-dried cherry tomatoes marinated in olive oil, herbs and garlic or any sun-dried tomato in oil

25g fresh basil (a small bunch)

300g mozzarella pearls/feta cubes

Wooden cocktail sticks

Olive oil for drizzling

Ground sea salt and ground black pepper for seasoning

SEMI-SUN-DRIED CHERRY TOMATO BREAD WITH ROCKET LEAVES, SALAMI AND ROASTED RED PEPPER

The semi-sun-dried cherry tomato bread is lovely and moist and works well with a combination of toppings to make these colourful, tasty starter bites. You can buy a jar of roasted red peppers if you do not have time to roast them yourself.

Method:

- Preheat the oven to 200°C/Gas Mark 7 and roast the red peppers until the skin gets black and charred. This takes about 30 minutes. When the peppers are blackened, place them in a small plastic bag until cool and then peel off the skin and deseed.
- Slice the roasted peppers into long slivers.
- Cut the bread into small slices and place them on a large platter. Place rocket leaves, a piece of salami and a sliver or two of roasted red pepper on top of each slice.
- Drizzle with olive oil and season with salt and black pepper before serving.

Ingredients:

2 red peppers

1 loaf sun-dried cherry tomato bread (see p. 131)

Rocket leaves

Salami slices

Olive oil for drizzling

Sea salt and ground pepper to season

WHOLEMEAL PESTO SCONE BITES

Adding a dollop of pesto to the brown scone mix gives them a lovely speckled fleck. They look beautiful topped with a slice of cucumber, cheese and drizzle of pesto and are a very filling bite that will take the edge off your hunger.

Method:

- Preheat the oven to 180°C/Gas Mark 6.
- Follow the instructions to make the brown scone mix, adding in 2 tbsp of pesto.
- Roll the dough to about 1cm thick. You want the bites thick enough so that you can slice them in two but not too thick as they are just a starter.
- Use a small round pastry cutter to make 30 mini scones.
- Bake them for 15 minutes.
- Leave the mini scones to cool on a wire tray.
- Wash and slice the cucumber and slice the cheese.
- Cut each mini scone in two and use a teaspoon to drizzle on some pesto.
- Add a piece of cheese and a slice of cucumber.
- Serve on a platter drizzled with some more pesto.

Ingredients: – makes 60

1 quantity of brown scone mix (see p. 135) with 2 tbsp of home-made pesto (see p. 45) added

1 cucumber

Some nice cheese, e.g. Carrigaline Farmhouse Garlic and Herb, Gubbeen, Wicklow Baun, etc.

Home-made pesto for topping

GOAT'S CHEESE, OLIVE AND RED ONION PUFF PASTRY BITES

Ideal as party bites these can be made in advance, frozen and then thawed out whenever you need them. Any leftovers can be used as lunchbox fillers. Remember to defrost the pastry in the fridge overnight. A great alternative to the red onion base is to use cranberry sauce perhaps with some bacon and brie.

Method:

- Defrost the pastry in the fridge overnight.
- Peel the red onions, then cut them in half and finely slice each half.
- Heat the olive oil in a large frying pan over a low heat and put the red onions on to soften for 15 minutes.
- Peel and crush the garlic and cut the olives in half and set aside.
- Chop the semi-sun-dried tomatoes into small pieces and set aside.
- Preheat the oven to 200°C/Gas Mark 7.
- Add the crushed garlic, balsamic vinegar and herbes de Provence to the onions and cook for 5 minutes. Then take off the heat and allow to cool while preparing the pastry.
- Unroll the pastry sheets and cut each into sixteen squares.
- Using a knife create a narrow border around the edge of each pastry square approximately 1cm wide, being careful not to cut right through the pastry – this will enable the pastry edge to puff up.
- Arrange a generous spoonful of the red onion mix on each pastry square, then a piece of goat's cheese topped with half an olive and some sun-dried tomato.
- Brush the edge of each square with a little beaten egg and milk mixed together.
- Bake the pastry squares for 15 minutes until puffed up and golden.
- Serve hot or cold, dressed with a drizzle of pesto and a scattering of finely chopped fresh parsley.

Ingredients: – makes 32

425g frozen puff pastry sheets
   (2 sheets in pack)

4 medium red onions

1 tbsp olive oil

2 garlic cloves

100g black olives (pitted)

50g semi-sun-dried tomatoes

2 tsp balsamic vinegar

1 tsp herbes de Provence

100g goat's cheese

1 egg and a little milk for glazing

Pesto and fresh parsley for
   garnishing

LAMB KOFTAS

These little morsels can be served hot or cold with cocktail sticks and a dip.

Method:

- Peel and grate the onion and set aside.
- Peel and crush the garlic and set aside.
- Rinse and finely chop the coriander and set aside.
- Lightly beat the egg and set aside.
- Use a fork to combine the grated onion, crushed garlic, coriander, beaten egg, cumin and thyme in a large bowl.
- Add the lamb and mix well with a fork. Season with a little salt and pepper.
- Shape into golf-ball-sized meatballs.
- Heat the olive oil on a large frying pan over a medium to high heat and cook the meatballs until brown on all sides – cut through one to check that they are cooked through and the juices are clear.
- Serve on cocktail sticks with a raita/ cucumber dip.

Ingredients: – makes around 30 depending on the size

1 large onion

2 garlic cloves

Handful of fresh coriander

1 egg

2 tsp ground cumin

2 tsp dried thyme

1kg minced lamb

Sea salt and ground pepper to season

2 tbsp olive oil

MOROCCAN COUSCOUS

Couscous is fattened up with plumped up raisins and given flavour and heat with some spice and the chilli powder. Crunchy peppers and cucumber give it more texture and it makes a wonderful side dish.

Method:

- Melt the butter in a saucepan over a low to medium heat.
- Add the couscous and cook for 2 minutes.
- Take off the heat and pour over the hot chicken stock. Cover the saucepan with cling film and leave to stand for 5 minutes.
- Remove the cling film, put back onto the heat, separate the couscous with a fork, and cook for 2 minutes.
- Deseed and chop the peppers into cubes, peel and cube the cucumber and add to the couscous.
- Heat the olive oil in a frying pan over a low heat and add the coriander, mild chilli powder and raisins and cook for a couple of minutes to plump up the raisins.
- Stir the white vinegar into the frying pan and mix with the raisin and spices.
- Pour the raisin mixture over the couscous and mix well.
- Finely chop the fresh coriander and parsley and mix through the couscous.

Ingredients: – serves 5–6

15g unsalted butter

250g couscous

250ml hot chicken stock from stock cube

2 peppers (1 red, 1 green)

Half a cucumber

125ml olive oil

2 tsp ground coriander

1 tsp mild chilli powder

Small handful of raisins

4 tbsp white wine vinegar

Small handful of fresh coriander

Small handful of fresh flat-leaf parsley

Note: Great served with Moroccan meatballs or as a BBQ side dish.

HOME-MADE COLESLAW

It's very easy to mix up a batch of coleslaw – just a little bit of grating, whip up the dressing and you are there. This can be made a day in advance and will keep well for two days stored covered in the fridge.

Ingredients: – serves 5–6

1 medium onion

1 medium carrot

1 small head of white cabbage

4 tbsp mayonnaise

1 tsp Dijon or wholegrain mustard

2 tsp olive oil

1 tbsp water

Method:

- Peel, halve and then finely chop the onion and place in a large bowl.
- Peel the carrot, cut the cabbage into quarters and cut out the hard stem piece.
- Use the coarse side of a grater to grate the carrot and cabbage into the bowl with the onion.
- Mix the mayonnaise, mustard and olive oil with the water, pour the mixture over the coleslaw, and stir well.

BABY POTATO SALAD

I recently rediscovered the joys of 'Heinz Salad Cream', which I'd probably last tasted in the 1980s. It makes the task of creating a tasty potato salad simple.

Ingredients: – serves 5–6

750g/1kg baby potatoes

3 spring onions

Small handful of chives

6 tbsp Heinz salad cream

Sea salt and ground pepper

Method:

- Wash, scrub and boil the potatoes in their skins in a saucepan of water.
- When cooked, drain the potatoes and roughly chop them into chunks with skins on.
- Rinse and chop the spring onions and the chives.
- Mix the spring onions, chives and Heinz salad cream with the potatoes until well coated. Season with ground sea salt and pepper.
- Serve cold as a side dish.

HONEY AND MUSTARD SALAD DRESSING

Use this to dress up some salad leaves, or to make a meal of it mix it up with leaves and some chopped chicken and rashers.

Ingredients:

1 heaped tsp wholegrain mustard

1 tbsp runny honey

2 tbsp extra virgin olive oil

1 tbsp white wine vinegar

Method:

- Pour all the ingredients into a small

jug or bowl and use a whisk to combine the dressing ingredients together.

BEETROOT, RED ONION, BABY LEAVES AND WALNUT SALAD

Beetroot and walnuts are high in nutrients, which makes this tasty salad very good for you. Vacuum-packed beetroot is cooked and ready to use and has no additives. Chopped walnuts are usually available in the baking section of the supermarket.

Ingredients: – serves 4–5

1 small red onion
250g vacuum-packed cooked beetroot
Baby salad leaves
2 tbsp chopped walnuts
Olive oil to drizzle
Sea salt and ground pepper to season

Method:

- Peel the red onion then cut it in half and finely slice it.
- Cut the beetroot into bite-size chunks.
- Put the salad leaves in a bowl with the beetroot, red onion and chopped walnuts.
- Serve drizzled with olive oil and seasoned with salt and pepper.

ASIAN SALAD AND DRESSING

This fresh, zingy salad is great with the Thai fishcakes recipe or a nice juicy steak.

Ingredients:

Mixed salad leaves (rocket, baby red leaf, mizuna, baby spinach)
Large bunch of coriander
1 red chilli
1 garlic clove
3cm thumb-width piece of ginger
1 lime
2 tbsp fish sauce (nam pla)
1 tbsp rice vinegar (or white wine vinegar)
3 tbsp sunflower oil

Method:

- Rinse the salad leaves and rinse and roughly chop the coriander.
- Deseed and finely chop the chilli.
- Peel and crush the garlic.
- Peel and grate the ginger.
- Zest the lime and then juice it.
- Put the chilli, garlic, ginger, lime zest and juice in a small jug and add the fish sauce, rice vinegar and sunflower oil and mix with a small whisk.
- Toss the salad leaves and chopped coriander in a bowl, drizzle over the dressing and toss again.

CHORIZO AND TOMATO SALAD

This dish is based on Jamie Oliver's *Jamie does Andalucía* programme and I make it using a local 'Gubbeen' chorizo. I've always known that my 'gob' meant my mouth but never gave the word's origins much thought. The name 'Gubbeen' is from the Gaelic *gobín*, meaning small mouthful, which refers to the bay where the farm is located in Schull, County Cork. Jamie uses sherry vinegar, which isn't available at my local supermarket, so I use red wine vinegar instead. This moves it away a little from its Spanish origins, but it still tastes great.

Method:

- Slice the chorizo.
- Heat the olive oil in a small frying pan and cook the chorizo over a medium heat for 5 minutes.
- Wash and slice the regular tomatoes and halve the cherry tomatoes.
- Peel and crush the garlic.
- Rinse and slice the spring onions.
- Chop up the basil.
- Add the garlic and red wine vinegar to the chorizo and cook for 2 minutes.
- Put the tomatoes in a bowl with the spring onion and basil, and pour over the chorizo and oil dressing from the pan.
- Mix well and serve.

Ingredients: – serves 5–6

180g chorizo – Gubbeen if you can get it

1 tbsp olive oil

400g mixture of regular and cherry tomatoes

1 garlic clove

2 spring onions

Small bunch of fresh basil

1 tbsp red wine vinegar

CARAMELISED RED ONION, CHERRY TOMATO AND MOZZARELLA TART

Puff pastry is tricky to make and as it's readily available in the freezer section of my supermarket I always buy it. Remember to leave the pastry in the fridge to defrost overnight. To speed things up you could caramelise the onions a couple of days before and keep them in a container in the fridge.

Method:

- Take the pastry sheets out of the fridge about 20 minutes before use.
- Preheat the oven to 200°C/Gas Mark 7.
- Peel, halve and thinly slice the red onion.
- Heat the olive oil over a low heat and gently cook the red onion for 10 minutes to soften.
- Add the balsamic vinegar and the muscovado sugar and raise the heat to vaporise the vinegar for 1 minute, reduce the heat and cook for 4 minutes and then set aside to cool.
- Heat two greased baking trays in the oven while rolling out the pastry on a lightly floured board.
- Rinse and cut the cherry tomatoes in half and roughly chop up the mozzarella.
- Place the pastry sheets on the heated baking trays and use a knife to score all the way around the edge of the pastry leaving a border about 1cm wide.
- Spread the red onion mix over the pastry, a little in from the edge. Add the halved cherry tomatoes and scatter the mozzarella cheese and mixed herbs on top.
- Brush the border of the pastry with beaten egg and milk.
- Bake for 15–20 minutes until golden.
- Serve hot with some dressed salad leaves.

Ingredients: – serves 8, 2 tarts each

425g frozen puff pastry sheets (2 sheets in pack – thawed overnight in fridge)

1 large red onion

1 tbsp olive oil

2 tbsp balsamic vinegar

2 tbsp muscovado sugar (or any brown sugar)

Butter to grease tray

Flour for dusting

20 cherry tomatoes

300g mozzarella

2 tsp mixed herbs

1 egg and a little milk

TOMATO AND HERB TART

This vegetarian summer tart is perfect for a light lunch with a salad. It's made on a large baking tray and will slice into at least 8 generous portions. If time is an issue make the pastry the night before.

Method:

- Make up the pastry and leave it to rest in the fridge for at least half an hour.
- Preheat the oven to 200°C/Gas Mark 7.
- Roll the pastry out on a floured board, and then use it to line a large baking tray lightly greased with butter.
- Prick the base of the pasty all over with a fork. Cover it with parchment paper weighed down with ceramic pie weights or dried beans or rice. Bake the pastry in the oven for 20 minutes.
- Rinse and halve the cherry tomatoes and slice the medium tomatoes.
- Whisk the eggs in a bowl and mix in the crème fraiche and pesto and season with salt and pepper.
- Pour the crème fraiche mixture onto the pastry and scatter the tomatoes on top.
- Sprinkle the herbs over the top. Bake the tart for 20 minutes.
- Serve slices of the warm tart straight from the baking tray with some dressed salad leaves.

Ingredients: – serves 8–12

1 quantity shortcrust pastry (see p. 160)

Flour to dust

Butter to grease tray

250g cherry tomatoes

4 medium tomatoes

3 eggs

200g crème fraiche

2 tbsp basil pesto

Sea salt and ground pepper

1 tsp herbes de Provence

BACON AND LEEK QUICHE

Quiche is good for casual entertaining all year round. I make two 20cm quiches from the shortcrust pastry. They are small but deeply filled and each one will yield five generous slices.

Ingredients: – serves 8–10

1 quantity shortcrust pastry (see p. 160)	8 eggs
Flour for dusting	3 tbsp Dijon mustard
Butter to grease tin	200ml cream
1 leek	250g Gruyère or any hard cheese (a combination of cheddar and Parmesan works well)
8 rashers (or leftover ham)	
40g unsalted butter	Sea salt and ground pepper

Method:

- Once the pastry has been rested, preheat the oven to 160°C/Gas Mark 4.
- Divide the pastry in two, roll each half out on a floured board and use to line two 20cm loose-bottomed greased cake tins. Try to have some pastry coming up over the edge of the tin to allow for shrinkage.
- Chill the pastry in the fridge for 15 minutes, then prick the base of the pastry with a fork, line it with parchment paper and fill with pie weights or dry beans.
- Bake blind in the preheated oven for 15 minutes. Remove the beans and parchment paper and return the pastry cases to the oven for 5–10 minutes, until very lightly coloured. While the pastry is baking blind, prepare the filling.
- Prepare the leek by cutting off the root and discarding any darker outer leaves. Slice the leek in half lengthways and rinse under a cold tap. Finely slice the leek and rinse it again in a colander (as the leek grows in layers dirt can get trapped in between).
- Chop the rashers with kitchen scissors. Melt the butter in a frying pan and gently fry the leek and rashers over a low to medium heat for 10 minutes until the leek softens.
- Whisk the eggs, Dijon mustard and cream together in a bowl.
- Grate the cheese and add to the egg mixture, season with salt and black pepper and add the leek and bacon. Pour into the part-baked pastry cases.
- Bake at 180°C/Gas Mark 6 for 25–30 minutes or until set and golden.

TIP: Prepare and bake your pastry cases in the morning and fill them when you need them. An alternative and equally good filling that I experimented with after Christmas was made by lining the pastry with half a jar of leftover cranberry sauce and using the leftover cooked ham instead of the rashers.

MOROCCAN MEATBALLS

Full of heady Moroccan spices, this dish brings meatballs to a new level.

Method:

- Peel and roughly chop the red onion, ginger and garlic, and blitz together with the deseeded chopped chilli, cumin and cinnamon in a mini chopper or food processor to create a spicy paste.
- Use a fork or your hands to mix the lamb with half of the spicy paste in a bowl and then shape them into meatballs the size of golfballs.
- Heat the olive oil in a large pan over a medium heat and brown the meatballs.
- Push the meatballs to the sides of the pan and cook the rest of the spicy paste in the centre of the pan for 1 minute.
- Add the plum tomatoes to the centre of the pan and roughly chop them with a knife. Add the chicken stock and stir to combine with the tomatoes, paste and meatballs.
- Bring to the boil then reduce to simmer for 25–30 minutes. (Test the centre of a meatball to check that it is cooked through.)
- Serve with a sprinkling of chopped fresh coriander and Moroccan couscous or rice.

Ingredients: – serves 6

1 large red onion

3cm thumb-width piece of ginger

3 garlic cloves

1 red chilli

2 tsp ground cumin

1 tsp ground cinnamon

800g minced lamb

1 tbsp olive oil

2 x 400g cans of plum tomatoes

250ml chicken stock

Handful of fresh coriander to garnish

CHICKEN CHASSEUR
– HUNTER'S CHICKEN

I love the depth of flavour that the tomato puree and wine bring to this simple dish. Humble chicken legs are rendered succulent in this classic French dish that takes 20 minutes to prepare and 1½ hours to cook.

Method:

- Preheat the oven to 180°C/Gas Mark 6.
- Heat the olive oil and half of the butter in a large casserole pan over a medium heat on the hob.
- Fry the chicken for 5 minutes on each side to lightly brown the skin and remove from the pan onto a plate.
- Meanwhile, peel and finely chop the shallots.
- Once the chicken has been removed, lower the heat, add the rest of the butter and gently fry the shallots for 5 minutes.
- Peel and crush the garlic and add to the shallots to cook for 1 minute.
- Wash the mushrooms and leave whole if they are small or cut in half or quarters if they are large. Add to the shallot and garlic and cook for 2 minutes.
- Stir well and then add the wine and the tomato puree, stir again, bring to the boil and then reduce the heat to allow the sauce to a simmer. Add the thyme sprigs and chicken stock and return the chicken and any juices to the pan.
- Put a lid on the casserole and place into the oven to cook for 1 hour until the chicken is tender.
- Serve with baby potatoes, some green beans and crusty bread to mop up the juices.

Ingredients – serves 6

1 tsp olive oil

25g unsalted butter (approx. 1 heaped tbsp)

6 chicken legs (with skin on)

4 shallots

2 garlic cloves

400g button mushrooms

300ml white wine

2 tbsp tomato puree

2 thyme sprigs or 1 tsp dried thyme

500ml chicken stock

Note: Chicken leg does not mean just the drumstick: it also includes the thigh, which has some of the most succulent meat on the chicken. This dish is a lot tastier made with these cuts than with more expensive breast meat.

CHICKEN PROVENÇAL

This dish sounds sophisticated, but it is simple to prepare and is ready in under 30 minutes.

Method:

- Put the flour on a large plate or in a bowl. Cut the chicken into bite-size pieces and toss it in the flour to lightly coat it.
- Peel and finely chop the onion and crush the garlic.
- Heat the olive oil in a large casserole pot over a medium heat, add the chicken pieces, chopped onion and crushed garlic, and cook for 5 minutes until lightly browned.
- Add the chopped tomatoes, herbes de Provence and wine, reduce the heat and cover to cook for 10 minutes.
- Cut the olives in half and stir these in to heat through.
- Scatter the basil leaves on top to garnish the dish when just about to serve.
- Serve with rice or baby potatoes and some crusty garlic bread.

Ingredients: – serves 5–6

2 tbsp flour

4 skinless chicken breasts

1 large onion

3 garlic cloves

2 tbsp olive oil

2 x 400g cans of chopped tomatoes

1 tsp herbes de Provence

500ml red wine

20 pitted black olives

Small bunch of fresh basil

CHICKEN AND MUSHROOMS IN A CREAMY WHITE WINE SAUCE

This indulgent dish should please most tastes and is very easy to make. You can make it ahead of time, refrigerate and then reheat it when needed.

Method:

- Chop the chicken into bite-size chunks.
- Heat the olive oil in a large saucepan and cook the chicken pieces for 5 minutes over a medium heat.
- Meanwhile, peel and finely chop the shallots and wash and slice the mushrooms.
- Push the chicken out to the sides of the pan and melt the butter in the centre and add the shallots, reduce the heat to low and leave to soften for 5 minutes.
- Add the sliced mushrooms and roughly chopped parsley and mix well with the onion as it cooks for 2 minutes.
- Add the white wine, mix everything, and bring to the boil.
- Add the chicken stock, mix well and reduce the heat to simmer for 15 minutes with a lid on stirring occasionally.
- Add the double cream, raise the heat and mix well until heated through.
- Serve with some boiled rice and a sprinkling of chopped parsley.

Ingredients: – serves 6–8

6 skinless chicken breasts

2 tbsp olive oil

4 shallots

400g mushrooms

25g unsalted butter

Few sprigs of curly parsley

250ml white wine

750ml chicken stock

220ml double cream

229

CHICKEN STUFFED WITH HERBY GOAT'S CHEESE IN PROSCIUTTO

This simple, tasty dish, which looks sophisticated, is ready in 30 minutes. It is perfect served with a leafy green salad or you could throw in some baby potatoes to roast alongside the chicken in their skins. When I cooked this dish with tarragon, the kids turned up their noses and didn't like what they called the aftertaste. Tarragon has a strong smell and when you chop it the fragrance is almost liquorice or antiseptic. Personally I thought the combination worked really well, but if you are in any doubt just go with the parsley.

Method:

- Preheat the oven to 200°C/Gas Mark 7.
- Finely chop the parsley or tarragon and zest one lemon.
- Place the goat's cheese in a bowl and mix in the herb and lemon zest with a fork.
- Use a sharp knife to cut a deep slit into the side of each chicken breast and stuff with 1–2 teaspoons of the herby goat's cheese mix.
- Wrap two slices of Prosciutto or Serrano ham around each chicken breast and secure with a cocktail stick or mini skewer.
- Drizzle the wrapped chicken with some olive oil and roast for 25 minutes, until cooked through.
- Serve with wedges of lemon and roasted baby potatoes or a green leafy salad.

Ingredients: – serves 4–5

Small handful of flat-leaf parsley or tarragon

2 lemons (1 for serving)

150g soft goat's cheese

4 skinless chicken breasts

8 slices of Prosciutto di Parma or Serrano ham

Cocktail sticks or skewers to secure

Olive oil to drizzle

BEEF BOURGUIGNON

The long, slow cooking time really tenderises the beef in this classic French dish. Traditional recipes use pancetta but as my supermarket doesn't stock it, I use streaky bacon instead. If you can get hold of a Burgundy red wine to slosh into this, all the better.

Method:

- Preheat the oven to 150°C/Gas Mark 3.
- Peel and finely slice the shallots.
- Peel and crush the garlic.
- Rinse the mushrooms and cut them in half if they are large.
- Heat the olive oil in a large casserole pot on the hob over a medium heat.
- Season the beef with salt and pepper, quickly brown it off for a couple of minutes, and then transfer it to a large plate.
- Use kitchen scissors to cut the streaky bacon into small pieces into the casserole pot and fry it along with the shallots, mushrooms and garlic for a few minutes.
- Add in the tomato puree and cook for 1 minute, stirring it into the mixture. Return the beef and juices to the casserole dish.
- Pour over the wine, bring to the boil and stir well.
- Add the bouquet garni to the casserole dish and transfer it to the preheated oven to cook slowly for 2½ hours.
- Remove the bouquet garni and serve with baby potatoes and garnish with a generous sprinkling of freshly chopped parsley.

Ingredients: – serves 6

10 small shallots

3 garlic cloves

400g button mushrooms

2 tbsp olive oil

1kg diced shin beef or any stewing beef

Sea salt and ground pepper

5 strips of streaky bacon

1 tbsp tomato puree

750ml bottle of red wine

1 bouquet garni (bay, thyme, parsley, rosemary tied together)

Fresh chopped parsley to garnish

BEEF AND RED WINE HOTPOT

This dish is ideal for entertaining. Stew tastes better on the second day as the beef is even more tender so you can make the stew element of this dish the day before. All that you will have to do is reheat it, prepare the potatoes and grate some Parmesan. Like a regular beef stew, any leftovers can be reheated and wrapped in pastry to make Cornish pasties.

Method:

Stew

- Peel and slice the shallots. Peel and slice the carrots into thin thumb-length batons. Peel and crush the garlic.
- Sprinkle the beef with the flour and mix well.
- Heat 2 tablespoons of the olive oil in a large casserole pot over a medium to high heat and brown the outside of the meat in batches placing the browned meat on a plate.
- Add the other 2 tablespoons of olive oil to the casserole pot mixing up any residue from the meat juices with a wooden spoon, lower the heat and add the shallots and carrots to cook for 10 minutes, with a lid on, until softened.
- Add the crushed garlic, cook for 1 minute, and mix well.
- Add the red wine and bring to the boil for 1 minute, then put back in the beef and any juices.
- Add the stock, bay leaves and thyme sprigs, and simmer on a low heat for 2 and a half hours, stirring occasionally.

Ingredients: – serves 8

Stew – make it the day before

10 small shallots

500g carrots

4 garlic cloves

1½kg diced shin beef

3 tbsp flour

4 tbsp olive oil

200ml red wine

750ml beef stock

2 bay leaves

3 thyme sprigs

Topping

800g potatoes

50g Parmesan

25g unsalted butter

On the day:

- Reheat the stew on the hob and divide it between two baking dishes, removing the bay leaves and thyme sprigs.
- Preheat the oven to 200°C/Gas Mark 7.

Topping

- Peel and thinly slice the potatoes and boil for 5–10 minutes until almost cooked. While they are cooking, grate the Parmesan.
- Drain the potatoes and add the butter, mixing it to melt and coat the slices.
- Layer the potatoes on top of the stew and sprinkle generously with the Parmesan. Bake for 30 minutes.
- Serve with some crusty bread to mop up the juices.

PLANNING FAMILY GATHERINGS AND PARTIES AT HOME

CONFIRMATIONS/COMMUNIONS/CHRISTENINGS

When you have a large number of people to entertain the following is a suggested menu for a rambling day of varied tastes, to suit all. Assuming that it's summer time and the weather is kind, a barbecue is definitely the way to go. You'll surely have at least one volunteer who will look after cooking the meat. Personally I wouldn't go to the bother of making home-made burgers for this, but would order them from the butcher instead. (Even if it's winter I still would go with burgers and butcher's sausages – start them off on the hob and finish them in the oven.)

You may have to cater for both lunch and dinner so I've included options for an early lunch of soup and savoury tart and quiche where the preparation for both can be almost completed the day before. Generally for a family and friends gathering there'll be a few people who will volunteer to help: let them bring a salad or a dessert and make things a bit easier for yourself.

LUNCH MENU

Mushroom soup
with brown bread

~

Savoury tart of puff
pastry, caramelised onions,
goat's cheese, cherry
tomatoes and basil

and/or Bacon and leek
quiche

Mixed salad leaves with
honey and mustard dressing

Coleslaw

Lemon cheesecake
Strawberry cheesecake
Pear tiramisu

EVENING MENU

Mini brown scone, cheese
and pesto bites

Chilli jam and salsa with
pitta chips

~

BBQ burgers and butcher's
sausages

Selection of salads

~

Cupcakes

236

PREPARATION AND SCHEDULE FOR COMMUNION, ETC. AT HOME

One Week Before

- Make four bacon and leek quiches, cool and freeze.
- Make four loaves of brown bread, cool and freeze.
- Make two batches of mini brown scones, cool and freeze.

Two Days Before

- Make up the caramelised onions for the base of the tart, store in a sealed container in the fridge.
- Make up the pesto, store in a sealed container in the fridge.
- Make up the cherry tomato and chilli jam and refrigerate.
- Make the cupcakes and store them in a sealed container.

One Day Before

- Make the mushroom soup and chill in the fridge.
- Make up some salads, e.g. Moroccan couscous, coleslaw, baby potato salad and refrigerate.
- Make up the honey and mustard salad dressing and refrigerate.
- Make up the cheesecakes and pear tiramisu and refrigerate.
- Ice the cupcakes and store them in a sealed container.
- Put the puff pastry and quiches in the fridge to defrost overnight.
- Leave the brown bread and mini brown scones out to defrost.

On the Day

Lunch:

- Assemble and bake the puff pastry tarts with the prepared caramelised onion base, cherry tomatoes, feta and basil.
- Reheat the soup and serve with brown bread.
- Reheat the quiches in the oven and serve with dressed salad leaves.

Evening:

- Prepare the pitta chips and serve with the chilli jam and salsa for dipping.
- Assemble the mini brown scone and pesto bites for nibbling on.
- Put out the salads and let everybody help themselves when the burgers and butcher's sausages are done.

237

CHILDREN'S BIRTHDAY PARTY

I'll say two things about having a children's party at home:

A) Boys will wreck your house

B) Girls will wreck your head

Once you know that and still want to cater at home, I'll tell you something else I've learned. In my experience (six kids – lots of parties), it costs less to have your party at an entertainment venue than to have it at home. Honestly, that's what I've found, plus you go home to a clean house with your head relatively unhassled.

Saying that, I have done it myself, and on one memorable occasion, whatever possessed me at the time, even went to the lengths of making home-made piñatas in the shape of Spider Pig and Bart from the Simpsons with a Homer-head-shaped birthday cake. My memories of the birthday parties at home will definitely stay with me a lot longer than the ones at the swimming pools, soccer halls or entertainment centres, so from that point of view I'm glad that I've done it.

On top of the suggested menu, I would stock up on crisps, sweets, ice-cream, ketchup, mayonnaise and fizzy drinks. I would gener-

KID'S BIRTHDAY PARTY MENU:

Chicken Nuggets
Potato Wedges
Cocktail Sausages
Coleslaw

NY Cupcakes
Chocolate and
Raspberry Birthday
Cake

ally stick to lemon and lime flavoured minerals as they're colourless which means less additives in your kids and less staining on your carpet.

Kids expect party bags going home stuffed with a bit of junk and perhaps a small toy.

You will also need: candles, balloons, streamers, music and entertainment. Bouncy castles are great if you have the weather for them, though they can be dangerous and require supervision. Ellie fell out of the bouncy castle and broke her arm at her Communion party!

If you wanted the kids to get involved with the food and have a bit of fun with it, pizza parties, where they roll their own dough and choose their own toppings, and cupcake parties, where they ice and decorate their own cupcakes, are a couple of options.

PREPARATION AND SCHEDULE FOR CHILDREN'S BIRTHDAY PARTY

Evening before

- Prepare and coat the chicken nuggets and chill them on baking trays covered in cling film. This is raw food and needs to be stored away from all other ready-to-eat foods.
- Bake the cake and store un-iced.
- Bake the cupcakes and store un-iced.

On the morning

- Make the coleslaw.
- Ice the cake and cupcakes.

When kids arrive

- Prepare the potato wedges.
- Start to cook the potato wedges, chicken nuggets and cocktail sausages half an hour after the kids arrive so that they will be eating halfway through the party.
- Try to get the kids to eat some hot food before they tuck into the junk.

COFFEE MORNING

Coffee mornings are a casual alternative to a dinner party if you just want to catch up with a few friends. There's nothing like home-baking and the menu here is simple. It's all about the chat really.

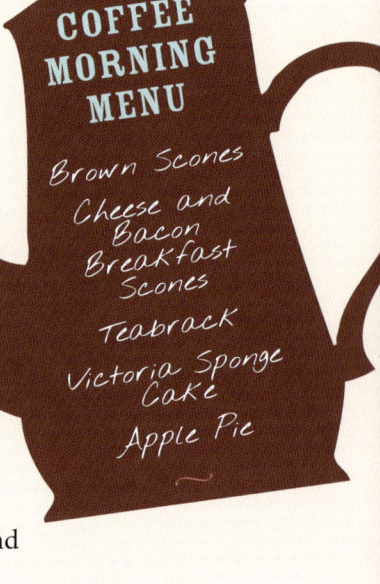

COFFEE MORNING MENU

Brown Scones

Cheese and Bacon Breakfast Scones

Teabrack

Victoria Sponge Cake

Apple Pie

PREPARATION AND SCHEDULE FOR COFFEE MORNING

One Week Before

- Bake, cool and freeze the brown scones and the cheese and bacon breakfast scones.

Night before

- Soak the fruit for the teabrack.
- Make the apple pie, leave to cool and store in a cool place.
- Put the scones into the fridge to defrost overnight.

On the morning (3 hours before)

- Bake the Victoria sponge cake and leave to cool.
- Bake the teabrack and leave to cool.

On the morning (1 hour before)

- Leave the scones out of the fridge to come to room temperature.
- Fill the Victoria sponge cake with jam and cream.

Serving up

- Warm the cheese and bacon scones in the oven or cut in half and warm under the grill.
- Serve the brown scones with butter, jam, cheese and relish.

GIRLS' NIGHT IN

No matter what age I am, when I get together with my girlfriends for a catch-up session in one of our homes we are always girls.

PREPARATION AND SCHEDULE FOR GIRLS' NIGHT IN

Night before

- Make the meringue base for the strawberry and hazelnut toffee pavlova and leave to cool in a dry place. Do not fill.
- Make up double the quantity of Indian chicken curry. Cool it and refrigerate it overnight.

On the evening (3 hours before)

- Make up the guacamole and salsa fresca and refrigerate them.
- Cut up the pitta breads for the pitta chips and put them on baking trays but do not oil or spice them yet.
- Fill the strawberry and hazelnut toffee pavlova and refrigerate it.

When the girls arrive

- Have some pistachio nuts out in bowls for nibbling.
- Oil and spice the pitta chips and put them in the oven.
- Put out the guacamole and salsa fresca for dipping the pitta chips into.
- Put the Indian chicken curry into one large or two medium saucepans and bring the heat up to almost boil, then simmer gently until needed and use quick boil-in-the-bag rice for convenience.

GIRLS' NIGHT IN MENU

Guacamole
Salsa Fresca
Pitta Chips
Indian Chicken Curry
with rice, naan bread
or chapattis

~

Strawberry and
Hazelnut
Toffee Pavlova

CHRISTMAS TURKEY DINNER PLANNER

As this is one of the most anticipated meals of the year, a little bit of planning will help to relieve the stress that surrounds producing a Christmas turkey dinner. What will also make a big difference is to delegate the jobs that you don't have to do yourself. Kids are great at peeling vegetables and setting the table etc. Get some Christmassy music going in the background, light some cranberry or mulled spice scented candles and sip a Bailey's on ice (or tipple of your own choice) to get yourself in the right frame of mind. It shouldn't be all about slaving and sweating in the kitchen on your own so make sure everyone knows it's Christmas for you as well. I think of a Christmas turkey dinner as an oversized roast chicken dinner with a few airs and graces.

Puff Pastry Bites iwth Cranberry Sauce, Bacon and Brie*

~

Roast Turkey and Roast Potatoes with Herb Stuffing and Gravy
Golden Syrup Baked Ham
Mashed Potatoes, Carrots, Sweetcorn and Brussel Sprouts

~

Black Forest Roulade

*Make, cool and freeze the puff pastry bites (see page 209) a week ahead, defrost in the fridge overnight and reheat in the oven.

Planning

- Work out what time you want to eat at and put that into the planner, then work backwards adjusting the times as per suggested times.
- If you are planning to eat at 2.30, tell everybody it's 3 p.m. – leaving a little leeway helps to take a bit of the pressure off.
- The timings recommended for cooking an unstuffed turkey on the Irish Safefood website are 19 minutes per kg + 124 minutes in a fan oven at 180°C or Gas Mark 5. They recommend covering the turkey with tinfoil to keep it juicy and basting it every hour, removing the tinfoil half an hour from the end to brown the skin. Based on this, the suggested timings here would be for a 6kg turkey (12 servings).
- The ham will require 20 minutes per 450g + 20 minutes extra.
- As you can see I keep my vegetable options simple: boiled and roast potatoes, carrots, Brussels sprouts and sweetcorn. Substitute these with whatever vegetables you fancy. When preparing the potatoes I peel them and leave them in cold water until required. This isn't ideal from a nutritional point of view, but with so much going on, they do need to be prepared in advance.

SCHEDULE
Christmas Eve

- Cook the spiced beef (a Cork tradition, spiced beef is bought pre-spiced by the butcher) – this takes 2 to 3 hours of simmering depending on the weight of the joint.
- Soak the ham in a pot in the fridge. As the ham is usually heavily salted, the risk is probably low if it is left out and unrefrigerated when the environs are cold. However, leaving it in a warm kitchen this could pose a risk, so it would be best practice to soak it in the fridge overnight. (Change the water before boiling the next day.) The ham can alternatively be cooked a day ahead, then slices reheated in the microwave when needed.
- Make the cranberry sauce. (Cranberries, sugar, water, orange zest. Bring them to the boil and reduce to simmer until the cranberries burst – 10 minutes. Cool and refrigerate.)

Planning Family Gatherings and Parties at Home

Christmas Day

	Suggested Times	Your Adjusted Times
Make Starter	9 a.m.	
Preheat the oven to 180°C	9.30 a.m.	
Set table	9.30 a.m.	
Ham on to boil	9.30 a.m.	
Prepare stuffing (don't cook yet)	9.30 a.m.	
Assemble salad	9.50 a.m.	
Ham to simmer	10 a.m.	
Turkey on to roast	10 a.m.	
Peel potatoes and cover in water	10.30 a.m.	
Potatoes on to parboil for 10 mins	1.20 p.m.	
Prep rind and glaze ham and roast	1.30 p.m.	
Potatoes on to boil	1.30 p.m.	
Potatoes on to roast	1.30 p.m.	
Stuffing on to cook	1.30 p.m.	
Prepare carrots and sprouts	1.40 p.m.	
Turkey and ham out to rest	2.00 p.m. (loosely cover with tinfoil)	
On with carrots	2.10 p.m.	
On with Brussels sprouts	2.10 p.m.	
On with frozen sweetcorn	2.15 p.m.	
Drain vegetables	2.20 p.m.	
Make gravy (use vegetable water to make up the gravy – see chicken gravy recipe for details, pp. 71–2)	2.20 p.m.	
Dinner is served	2.30 p.m.	

YOUR NOTES AND RECIPES

ACKNOWLEDGEMENTS

Huge thanks to my family and friends for your support and encouragement, especially Deirdre Lee for inspiring this book and encouraging me.

Thank you too to the team at Mercier Press, especially Mary, Patrick, Catherine, Sharon, Barbara and Wendy, for believing in this book and guiding me every step of the way.

Finally a big shout-out of thanks to my fellow Irish Food Bloggers, members of the Irish Food Bloggers Association, Facebook Fans and Twitter followers for making me feel at home in cyberspace and sharing your world with me.

INDEX

Index

Index

MERCIER PRESS
Cork
www.mercierpress.ie

© Sheila Kiely, 2012
Food Styling and Photography © Sheila Kiely, 2012

ISBN: 978 1 85635 880 4

10 9 8 7 6 5 4 3 2 1

Designed by Twibill Design, Cork.

A CIP record for this title is available from the British Library

This book is sold subject to the condition that it shall not, by way of trade or otherwise, be lent, resold, hired out or otherwise circulated without the publisher's prior consent in any form of binding or cover other than that in which it is published and without a similar condition including this condition being imposed on the subsequent purchaser.

No part of this publication may be reproduced or transmitted in any form or by any means, electronic or mechanical, including photocopying, recording or any information or retrieval system, without the prior permission of the publisher in writing.

Printed and bound in the EU.